TT2007

Mick Duckworth

COMMISSIONING EDITOR Miles Cowsill

DESIGNED BY Tracey Harding

PUBLISHED BY Lily Publications in 2007

Lily Publications
Limited

© 2007 Lily Publications Ltd,
PO Box 33, Ramsey, Isle of Man, IM99 4LP
Tel 01624 898446 Fax 01624 898449

WEB www.lilypublications.co.uk **EMAIL** lilypubs@manx.net

ISBN 978 1 89960203 2

The publishers are grateful to the following for providing images
for this book:

ANDREW BARTON   STEPHEN HARDING
CAROL BASNETT   TRACEY HARDING
STAN BASNETT   JACKIE HORNE
MILES COWSILL   MANX NATIONAL HERITAGE
TIMOTHY COWSILL   MODDEY DHOO MCC
DAVE COLLISTER   CHRIS MOLYNEUX
DOUBLE RED   MCN
BARRY EDWARDS   SIMON PARK
FOTTOFINDERS   BERNHARD WEBER
IAN HARLAND   ADY GELL
                         ALSO AUTHOR'S COLLECTION

TITLE PAGE

**Sign of the times: John McGuinness set the first 130mph lap of
the Mountain Course during his winning Senior TT ride.** DAVE COLLISTER

**The magnificent silver statuette of Mercury, speedy messenger
of the gods, was presented to the Auto-Cycle Club by the Marquis
de Mouzilly St Mars 100 years ago.** DOUBLE RED

CONTENTS

Introduction BY MICK DUCKWORTH

The author at work talking to John McGuinness. LILY PUBLICATIONS

Nothing on earth is quite like the Isle of Man TT. No other motorcycle race is held on such a challenging circuit as the 37.73-mile Mountain Course and few sporting events of any kind have traditions and legends as rich as the TT's.

This year marks the 100th anniversary of the first Tourist Trophy motorcycle race, held on the Isle of Man because its semi-autonomous government could close public roads for motor sport.

That first TT of 1907 was held on a lowlands circuit, as the Snaefell Mountain Road used for car racing was thought too severe for the motorcycles of the time. But makers soon developed stronger engines and multi-speed transmissions. By 1911 the two-wheeler TT was ready to climb the Island's central hills and after a break during World War One, the present Mountain Course route was adopted.

Today, the problem is not so much about having power, but being able to use and control the colossal output from modern engines. Manx roads are wider now, but they still twist, turn and undulate endlessly, while in places vicious bumps have formed on soft foundations. Suspension settings and tyre compounds are critical at 180mph and so, of course, are the riders' skills and powers of concentration. More than in any other motorcycle race, miscalculation can exact the ultimate penalty.

TT racing gets a grip on people: not just the competitors, who find it provides challenge and exhilaration in equal measure, but the fans who return year after year. For many Manx people, TT fortnight is a bright spot in the year that comes round as surely as Christmas or Easter.

During its long life the TT has faced many difficulties, so reaching the 100-year mark was cause for great celebration.

When Lily Publications proposed that we assemble an account of the Centenary TT to follow up TT100, the official history of the races, I did not need further prompting. A production like this is very much a team job, so I want to stress my gratitude to everyone listed below.

Mick Duckworth

Special thanks from the author

TO THE FOLLOWING, WHOSE HELP WAS INVALUABLE IN COMPILING THIS BOOK:

Trevor Barrett, Stan Basnett, Dave Collister, Miles Cowsill, Timothy Cowsill, Duke Video, Stephen Harding, Tracey Harding, Helen Hyde, IoM Department of Tourism and Leisure, Derry Kissack, Manx Motor Cycle Club, Bill Snelling at FoTTofinders, Southern 100 MCRC, Andy Sykes, Dot Tilbury of IoM Post, TT Riders Association, the TT Marshals Association and the TT Supporters Club, Vintage Motor Cycle Club, and Murray Walker. An extra special thanks to my wife Irene for her patience during the production of this book.

Thanks also to all TT riders, officials, enthusiasts and everyone else who gave time to be interviewed during my researches.

The TT – a unique survivor

Trying the 1000cc MV Agusta Superbike racer for size. DAVE COLLISTER

Foreword by **Murray Walker**

It is a quite incredible achievement for any sporting event to have survived for 100 years, despite two world wars, a major financial recession and an outbreak of foot and mouth disease. Yet that is what the Isle of Man TT has done. And it is a measure of the event's uniqueness and charisma that it has outlasted the only other autosport events that I would put in the same category: the Mille Miglia and Targa Florio, two fabulous long-distance car races that were once run on Italian roads.

The TT's survival is a remarkable tribute to the Manx Government, which has supported it through thick and thin, as well as the inhabitants of the Island who have at best shown great enthusiasm for the races and at worst incredible tolerance.

No other motor sport event attracts people in great numbers for an entire period of two weeks and it must surely be unique that a whole place becomes a sporting happening in itself, where people are universally good-natured and in good humour. At the Centenary TT of 2007 the police reported that there were more than 50,000 motorcyclists and 20,000 bikes on the Isle of Man – and no trouble at all.

My own love of the TT goes back to the Twenties, when I was first taken to the Island as a toddler by my mother and father. Dad was a factory rider and we stayed each year at the Castle Mona, so I was in a privileged position and able to meet many of the top TT heroes of the day. When I was older I would bring my bike over to ride round the Course, just as people do today.

I did my first BBC commentary, festooned with microphone wires, standing on the slip road at Ballacraine in 1949. Later I broadcast from the phone box opposite the Highlander pub, from a road menders hut by the Central Hotel in Parliament Square, Ramsey and at Creg-ny-Baa.

My most vivid memory of commentating in the Fifties is from the 1957 Senior. I was at Creg-ny-Baa and Bob McIntyre came by on his Gilera closely followed by John Surtees on the MV Agusta, also a four-cylinder machine. The sound of those two accelerating away down the long straight, each changing up at different times was pure music!

There was a special magic about the many works teams that used to compete: AJS, BMW, Guzzi, Matchless, Mondial, Norton, NSU and others, as well as Gilera and MV. I used to love going round the garages to see all the riders and can remember visiting Honda when they were new to the TT.

In the early Sixties I took over the main commentary point at the Grandstand and was there until the BBC decided to discontinue broadcasts, mainly because the TT had lost its world status. I became very busy with the Formula One world and rather lost touch with the TT, but was aware that it seemed to be in terminal decline.

Returning for this year's centenary, I was struck by the changes in the Grandstand area and enormously impressed by the advanced technology, with instant, computerised timing and screens in the press centre offering constantly updated information.

Looking around in 2007, I got the strong impression that the TT is in the ascendant again.

Such an important event as the Centenary TT deserves to be recorded for posterity, which it so vividly is in this splendid book. It's all here: practising, racing, the people and the myriad other many facets of the whole two-week festival, day by day, rain or shine. So read on and enjoy!

Murray signing autographs beside the TT start line.
DAVE COLLISTER

Happy 100th

Real road racing: John McGuinness, the fastest TT racer ever, speeds through Kirk Michael village on his 1000cc Honda. DAVE COLLISTER

On a cool, breezy day in May 1907, the first Tourist Trophy race for motorcycles was run over closed public roads on the Isle of Man. Eleven out of the twenty-five starters finished and the winner averaged 38mph, boosting his speed by pedalling out of corners and up hills.

The idea of the 160-mile race was to encourage manufacturers to improve the speed, reliability and roadholding of their products. The organising Auto Cycle Club considered the 1907 experiment a success and decided to make the Tourist Trophy an annual event.

Little did those motorcycling pioneers realise what they had started. Could they have possibly imagined that the TT would still be going 100 years later, with machines from the world's leading factories racing on Manx public highways at speeds up to 200mph?

Even from the earliest times, pessimists said the Tourist Trophy would not last. As speeds rose and the dangers increased, there were calls for the racing to be banned, or at least moved to a safer purpose-built track. But the Isle of Man TT survived, only temporarily interrupted by two world wars and a foot and mouth epidemic.

Eventually the 37.73-mile Mountain Course, used for TT racing from 1911, went from providing the model for other international road races to being seen as an anomaly: too long, too difficult to learn quickly and impossible to make safe.

The Isle of Man was divorced from the international grand prix series in 1977, but it received a huge lift in the following year when popular 12-times winner Mike Hailwood made an astonishingly successful comeback. Gradually managing to re-invent itself, the TT evolved into a more varied motorcycling festival. The racing remained the main focus, but was increasingly seen as a distinct area of motorcycle racing, unlike massed-start on closed circuits with wide run-off areas.

Tourist Trophy!

2007 **TT Races**

Bennetts Superbike TT
Machines must comply with standing World Superbike and British Superbike rules (with specific TT amendments)

Four-strokes engines:
751cc-1000cc four cylinders
751cc-1000cc four cylinders
801cc-1000cc twin cylinders

PokerStars Superstock TT
Production formula allowing few modifications; machines must comply with standing FIM Superstock and MCRCB (UK) Superstock rules

Four-strokes engines:
600cc-1000cc four cylinders
750cc-1000cc three cylinders
851cc-1200cc twin cylinders

PokerStars Supersport TT
Machines must comply with standing FIM Supersport and MCRCB Supersport rules

Four-stroke engines:
401cc-600cc four cylinders
600cc-675cc three cylinders
600cc-750cc twin cylinders

The Senior TT, sponsored by PokerStars
Open to machines complying with the other solo TT classes and others at the organisers' discretion.

Bavaria Sidecar TT Race A and Bavaria Sidecar TT Race B
Three-wheeled machines carrying a driver and passenger complying with Formula Two Sidecar rules as specified in TT regulations

There were difficult times at the turn of the century. In 2000 Joey Dunlop, the unrivalled 26-times winner who personified the TT spirit for thousands of fans, was killed racing elsewhere. Then foot and mouth caused the one and only TT cancellation in 2001 and two years later the death of hugely popular David Jefferies, winner of nine races between 1999 and 2002, in a practice crash dealt the TT a heavy blow.

In 2004, the Manx Motor Cycle Club, organisers of the late-summer Manx Grand Prix since 1930 and before that the Amateur TTs of 1923-1929, took over organisation of the TT under a 20-year agreement between the Isle of Man Government and the ACU (Auto Cycle Union, formerly the Auto Cycle Club).

Fears that the TT was becoming a 'super Manx Grand Prix' for unknown British and Irish amateurs were addressed when the Department of Tourism and Leisure, the arm of Isle of Man government which promotes the TT, swung into action with a pro-active policy.

It was led by Tourism Minister David Cretney, a lifelong racing enthusiast. His lieutenants were rider liaison officers Richard 'Milky' Quayle, a TT winner retired from competitive riding, and Paul Phillips, later appointed the Island's director of motorsports. They literally went out looking for potential TT competitors at other events, on the nearby Irish public roads circuits and as far afield as the Macau GP in China.

Another objective was to maintain high quality fields of competitors, eliminating slower 'holiday racers' presenting a danger to those riding 'on the pace'.

A programme shakedown created the present format of four distinct solo races, and two sidecar races. The solo races are run to worldwide machine formulae based on homologated production models of 600cc and over. The disappearance of pure grand prix-type machines is mourned by many, but racing roadster-based machines is arguably truer to the original Tourist Trophy ideal. There is a case for racing smaller-capacity

Leaving the line. Top rider Ian Hutchinson has a low number.

DOUBLE RED

A feature peculiar to TT racing is the starting procedure. Riders are set off individually at 10-second intervals and so race as much against the clock as directly with each other. Computerised timing adopted in recent years is very accurate and apparently dead reliable.

The fastest riders are given the lowest 20 or so starting numbers and the better-known have their own 'trademark' numbers: for example John McGuinness races with Number 3, which his hero Joey Dunlop used in his later TT career. Following practice, fast riders with higher numbers may be moved up the field, filling places left by non-starters. Riders with early numbers have fewer problems getting past slower riders in front of them. Riders are not expected to carry 'unlucky' 13 if they don't wish to and from 1937 to 1981 the number was not used at all.

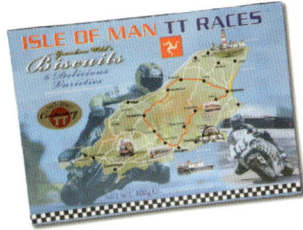

machines, however, especially for familiarising novices to Mountain Course racing.

Following a general election on the Island in 2006, Tourism Minister Cretney was replaced by Adrian Earnshaw, also an active motorcyclist.

Providing sufficient numbers of trained volunteer marshals to cover 37.73miles of road for every race and practice is key to the TT's well-being. Marshalling standards were strongly criticised in 2005, when four racing fatalities included a marshal and the rider who had collided with her at high speed. Under strong leadership from chief marshal Roger Hurst, the TT Marshals Association took the criticism on board and addressed it.

Glorious weather, record speeds and outstanding rides by young newcomers helped to give the 2006 TT a fresh, more positive, atmosphere and set the scene for The Big One in Centenary year.

Two riders with winning potential were declared non-starters before practising started.

Australian Cameron Donald, who lapped at 129mph in the 2006 Senior to finish second in his first TT year, was sidelined by an injury from a crash at Ireland's North West 200 races in May.

Jason Griffiths, a Welsh-born Island resident with 13 top-three finishes to his credit, decided to miss the TT to concentrate on his business.

Chief timekeeper Kevin Brookes (with beard) makes sure each riders' transponder is correlated to his allotted number and its class colour. Each transponder sends a unique digital signal to loops under the road at the start/finish line and other points at intervals around the Course. A new feature this year was a pair of loops recording riders' speed at the eastern end of the mile-long Sulby Straight.

CAROL BASNETT

Carpeted quarters. DOUBLE RED

The top teams

AIM YAMAHA   Rider: **Steve Plater**

ALPHA BOILERS/KLAFFI HONDA   Rider: **Martin Finnegan, Sidecar driver Klaus Klaffenbock**

BOLLIGER KAWASAKI   Riders: **Gary Carswell, Michael Weynand**

HM PLANT HONDA   Riders: **Ian Hutchinson, John McGuinness** (Superbike and Superstock)

HYDREX HONDA   Rider: **Guy Martin**

JMF MILLSPORT YAMAHA   Riders: **Conor Cummins, Nigel Beattie**

MSS DISCOVERY KAWASAKI   Rider: **Michael Rutter**

RELENTLESS SUZUKI BY TAS   Riders: **Adrian Archibald, Bruce Anstey**

STOBART HONDA   Rider: **Ian Lougher** (Superbike, Superstock)

TEAM BLACK HORSE RACING HONDA   Rider: **Ian Lougher** (Supersport), **Jimmy Moore**

UEL DUNCAN/ROBINSON CONCRETE HONDA   Rider: **Keith Amor**

The Island prepares

Making sure that the Mountain Course is in fit condition for the TT is a major task. It involves collaboration between the Island's highways authority, the Manx Motor Cycle Club which organises the racing, and the Auto Cycle Union, the sport governing body that issues a permit to run the TT.

A significant alteration was made to the Course over the winter months. Brandish Corner, named after Walter Brandish who crashed heavily there in 1922, is a left-hander following a fast, almost straight, stretch on the Mountain descent. It was made a gentler corner and the inside bank removed to improve visibility. The work was done to improve day-to-day road safety, but inevitably made the corner faster for racing. With the lap record standing at 129.451mph, there were suggestions – denied by the Highways chief – that it was a ploy to ensure a milestone 130mph lap would be achieved in Centenary year.

There were more subtle changes elsewhere. There are no cat's-eye reflectors along the centre-lines of roads that make up the Course, for obvious reasons: even the paint used for white lines is a special non-slip type. But cat's-eyes are used at the verges in some places and in 2006 fast riders were catching the knee-slider blocks attached to their leathers on them. For 2007, special flush-fitting solar-powered lights were put in place, to ensure that the ACU permit would be granted.

Finishing touches for the wooden manually-operated TT scoreboard facing the Grandstand, first used in the Twenties. **DOUBLE RED**

Cone convoys

Implementing the Mountain Road one-way system would involve a staff of more than 100. A number of temporary signs and the 2,000 traffic cones bought for the purpose had to be put in place, removed again for practice and race periods and then replaced afterwards. The job was executed by two convoys of hired motorway cone-laying trucks and road-sweeping vehicles. One was stationed at The Bungalow, roughly midway along the Mountain section, and the other at Ramsey. STAN BASNETT

The TT Grandstand area, not much improved since being rebuilt in the Eighties, benefited from a thorough spring clean by a volunteer team led by Paul Phillips and 'Milky' Quayle. Even farmers with land adjoining the Course were urged to help make the place look at its best for the occasion.

The entire Isle of Man Constabulary is always on red alert for the TT and with greater numbers of visitors and motorcycles than ever expected for the Centenary, the emphasis was on road safety.

After much deliberation, it was decided that the entire Mountain Road section of the Course, from Ramsey Hairpin to Creg-ny-Baa, should be a one-way system in the direction of the racing for the whole TT period. Previously only tried on Mad Sunday, the day when road riders traditionally emulate the racers by thrashing round the Course, the measure eliminates the risk of head-on collisions.

As usual, all leave was cancelled for the Island's 236-strong police force and re-enforcements brought in. Two traffic cops came from Germany to help overcome possible language problems, 12 officers were seconded from Jersey, one from the Irish Republic and 20 special constables were deployed.

Officers on foot would patrol crowded Douglas Promenade in the evenings backed up by CCTV cameras loaned by the UK Home Office and an alcohol ban would be enforced, except in specified areas where bars would operate. The police were hoping that they wouldn't have too many serious public order offences to deal with, as their custody facilities are limited.

Putting up straw bags. STAN BASNETT

Traditionally the Island's force has found that a relaxed, non-aggressive approach works best at TT time. But speed limits have multiplied on Manx roads in recent years and they are vigorously enforced: 15-20 bookings a day is normal and fines can be stiff. Driving bans issued on the Isle of Man now apply in the UK as well.

While the prospect of a bumper TT was clearly good news for the Island's shopkeepers, restaurateurs and brewers, it highlighted the shortage of hotel and guesthouse accommodation. The Homestay scheme, where households become temporary B&B establishments, was set up several years ago to address the problem and the normal figure of around 500 registered participants trebled for the Centenary.

Campsites were enlarged and new sites set up, while three football clubs offered space to cope with the 20,000 campers expected. More comfortable accommodation was at a premium, especially when plans for a 'floating hotel' on a cruise liner at Douglas fell through. Potential visitors were certainly lost: for example, a large American organisation dropped plans for a corporate trip when it could not find suitable accommodation.

The Island suffers from peak time road congestion on main routes in normal times, so the influx of thousands of motorcycles, the closure of roads and the simultaneous staging of a music festival threatened to cause serious problems. The Manx Government's idea for cutting congestion was to encourage commuters to use public transport: not just buses, but the Victorian steam railway in the south of the Island and the venerable Manx Electric railway connecting Douglas, Laxey and Ramsey. Additional trains and trams were laid on at a cost of £12,000.

Straw bags are gradually being replaced by FIM approved foam filled safety barriers. STAN BASNETT

New, safer, reflector. STAN BASNETT

Course furniture master plan. STAN BASNETT

Staying the Course

A special TT exhibition at the Manx Museum in Douglas was widely praised for its interesting and varied content. Called Staying the Course, the show was opened by Fifties' TT star and six-times world champion Geoff Duke before the TT festival, to run throughout the summer.

The museum's curator of social history Matthew Richardson sourced material from all over the world, from small items of memorabilia to machines that have won TT races at different times in its 100-year history.

Bikes on display included the well-preserved disc-braked Douglas twin on which Tom Sheard became the first Manxman to win a TT in the 1923 Senior, the Kawasaki KR750 on which Mick Grant won the 1977 Classic at an average of more than 110mph and Joey Dunlop's 1991 600cc Honda.

Also on show were the burnt-out remains of the sidecar outfit on which local hero Dave Molyneux had a spectacular crash at Rhencullen in practice for the 2006 races. TT clothing from different periods ranged from leathers and helmets worn by some of the most famous riders in TT history to early racing number bibs, and kit supplied to marshals and other officials. There was a mass of other memorabilia, from trophies and medals to a camping stove and copper kettle regularly used by a TT doctor eighty years ago.

The rich variety of exhibits was laid out decade by decade. MANX NATIONAL HERITAGE

Pavement artists

Two of Britain's best known artists specialising in motorcycle sport, Peter Hearsey and Rod Organ, held a joint exhibition during the TT period. Called TT100 Heroes and History, the show was at the Courtyard Gallery in the Tynwald Mills Centre near St John's. Douglas resident Peter Hearsey's paintings and prints capture the essence of speed, while Rod Organ, official artist to Ducati and the TT Riders Association, has been well known as a motorcycle artist for decades.

A TT Centenary mural by art students at the Isle of Man College brightened building site hoardings on the Promenade. TRACEY HARDING

Geoff Duke opens the exhibition. DAVE COLLISTER

How long?

As the length of the TT Course was set officially at 37.73 miles in the Thirties, it has been assumed that the many changes made to the roads since must have shortened it significantly. The Island's TT News made its own check on the true distance this year, when a racing cyclist rode the Course when the roads were quiet, keeping near the centre of the carriageway where possible. His instruments indicated 37.7224 miles – remarkably close to the official figure.

More Course alterations are due. The road layout at Braddan Bridge is being changed to incorporate two roundabouts, but the racing line should be unaffected. However, planned alterations on the approach to, and the exit from, Governor's Bridge are likely to make a difference for TT riders.

Centenary of Scouting

It wasn't only the TT's Centenary. The Scouts movement, founded in 1907, was also celebrating 100 years of existence. Scouts have been involved with the races since the earliest times, providing semaphore communications on the original St John's Course and later manually operating the scoreboard opposite the Grandstand. Yamaha sponsored the scoreboard Scouts in Centenary year and donated a 2007 YZF600 for a fund-raising tombola.

The joint anniversary was marked by a visit from the Chief Scout, TV presenter and actor Peter Duncan. He flew in on Senior race day to present the Harry Butterworth Trophy, given to the troop which performed best at the previous year's TT and Manx GP. The bronze trophy is awarded in memory of a former scoreboard controller who worked closely with the Scouts.

LEFT TO RIGHT
July 19 2007: Scouts tombola winner Paul Mulhurn (on the Yamaha R6 prize bike) is congratulated by Simon Belton of Yamaha. Others present at the handover outside Douglas dealer Road & Track Motorcycles are Harley Shimmin LEFT and Alan Teare of the Isle of Man Scouts Association. LILY PUBLICATIONS

Japanese helmet manufacturer Arai, one of the 2007 TT's sponsors, produced a official Centenary version of its upmarket RX-7 Corsair in a limited edition of 750, priced at £535. The Nitro helmet brand also released its own TT Centenary design, based on its N1610 type and priced at £115. TRACEY HARDING

Shops stocked up with TT merchandise and several special window displays enlivened the streets of Douglas. This one is at Bradford & Bingley International, sponsors of Island-based trials and stunt riding star Steve Colley. LILY PUBLICATIONS

Practical angels

Shortly before the TT, pupils at Ballakermeen High School in Douglas launched the Paddock Angels charity with £100 raised by selling cakes and holding a raffle. The aim of the charity is to offer practical help to TT competitors or other visitors who find themselves stranded on the Isle of Man by injury.

The TT transforms Douglas Promenade. BARRY EDWARDS

Raising spars to support the giant
Valhalla Marquee. STAN BASNETT

Peel Rocks

A new event overlapped with the 2007 TT period: the Peel Bay Festival held over seven evenings from May 30 to June 5. The £2m musical extravaganza was promoted by Jonathan Irving of local property company Street Heritage and put together by John Shakespeare who booked top-class names, including The Who, McFly, Sugarbabes and Madness. Bands from the vibrant local music scene were engaged as support acts.

The venue, an imposing temporary structure called the Valhalla Marquee, appeared on the skyline at Ballagyr to the north of Peel during the week before TT practice started. A water supply was laid on and arrangements made to avoid traffic and parking problems in the area.

Britain's biggest temporary building
dwarfs houses and trees. TRACEY HARDING

Off to a

Follow the leader: newcomers behind a travelling marshal. LILY PUBLICATIONS

A flypast by three preserved World War Two RAF aircraft from the Battle of Britain Memorial Flight marked the beginning of TT fortnight. The thundering four-engined Avro Lancaster heavy bomber PA474 thundered over Douglas Bay, escorted by two fighters; a Supermarine Spitfire MkVB and Hawker Hurricane LF363.

The planes had taken off from Blackpool and intended to return there, but because of an adverse weather forecast, the trio were directed to return directly to the BBMF's base at RAF Coningsby in Lincolnshire.

The Lancaster, piloted on this occasion by Squadron Leader Stuart Reid, is one of only two preserved in flying condition: the other is based in Canada. The Memorial Flight, which makes scores of special appearances annually, celebrated 50 years of aerial displays this year.

The last flying Avro Lancaster in Europe roars over the Queens Promenade in Douglas flanked by a Hurricane and a Spitfire. DAVE COLLISTER

flying start

Setting off on the learning lap. First-timers must wear high visibility vests during practice. DAVE COLLISTER

Although grey clouds hung over the Island by Saturday evening, practice for the Centenary TT got under way on time at 6.15pm. To help emphasise to competitors that the first session is intended for Course familiarisation and machine assessment, it is not officially timed.

The newcomers were set off first, escorted by travelling marshals who showed them the correct lines. The sixteen 'rookies' wearing orange visibility vests over their leathers were led by two riders new to the Mountain Course, but with plenty of racing experience under their belts.

One was Lincolnshire's Steve Plater (35), riding for AIM Yamaha. A winner of four rounds in the tough British Superbike series, he came to the TT fresh from a victory in the main event at the North West 200, run on public roads in Northern Ireland. Like other newcomers, he had done plenty of learning laps on open roads.

"I didn't mind being shown round by marshals. It helped me feel less nervous," Steve said.

The other leading newcomer was Scot Keith Amor (also 35), who shot to prominence by lapping the Dundrod Ulster GP roads course near Belfast at more than 126mph in 2006. That gained him a place in Uel Duncan's Honda-backed Robinson's Concrete team where he was promoted to Number One by the absence of Australian TT racing phenomenon Cameron Donald, injured at the North West 200.

Swedish Superbike star Kirste Miinin practiced briefly at the TT in 2005, but withdrew when his friend Joakim Karlsson was killed. On his return this year he was happy to be technically classed as a newcomer. But his Martin Bullock Racing Suzuki stalled as the pack set off, so he got his own personal guided tour behind chief travelling marshal Dick Cassidy later in the session.

Douglas taxi driver Barry Wood didn't need showing round as he's been racing on the Mountain Course since 1988. Even so, he came unstuck during the session, proving that Manx roads are always ready to bite the unwary. Barry (43) crashed at the second right-hand bend at Waterworks on the Mountain climb, where both he and his bike went clear over the wall and dropped several metres into gorse bushes. He was hospitalised with broken ribs, damaged vertebrae and a fractured left arm.

Three-times TT winner Adrian Archibald of the Relentless Suzuki by TAS equipe toured back to Douglas via Laxey on the coast road after one of his clip-on handlebars loosened at Ginger Hall.

Dave Molyneux was due to make his return to Sidecar TT racing after an horrific practice crash last year, but the 11-times winner failed to make the session. He was trying out his new outfit and its factory-kitted Honda CBR600 engine prior to practice at the Jurby testing area when a connecting rod broke loose at high rpm, causing mechanical carnage.

Even the most seasoned TT riders were newcomers to Brandish Corner as it's taken on closed roads.

"We're now going through there in fourth gear instead of second and it could be worth up to four seconds off a lap, but I don't expect to have it sorted until later in the week," John McGuinness said. Coming to the 2007 TT as the lap record holder with an average speed of 129.451mph set in 2006, the HM Plant Honda rider was not only a clear favourite for Centenary wins, but also, as he was well aware, expectations were high for the first 130mph lap. To achieve it, he needed to gain just over four seconds.

In the absence of official times from the computerised system operated by IT specialist Unysis, riders' friends and helpers were operating their own stop watches. Some claimed 118mph laps but speeds were moderated by rain squalls across the northerly parts of the course and the Mountain section.

The 10-mile one-way system was put in place for the fortnight, but the process took the police much longer than anticipated. Although the Mountain Road had been scheduled to re-open at 11.30am, the job was not completed until nearer 4pm.

Flags warned of damp patches. TRACEY HARDING

Roy Hanks, a Sidecar TT competitor since 1966, sweeps round Quarterbridge. The small red box visible in the main air intake is the transponder used for electronic timing. DAVE COLLISTER

Pre-TT
Classic races

Practising for the Pre-TT races on the Billown Circuit near Castletown: Nigel Smith and passenger Kris Hibberd at Church Bends on their Sixties-style sidecar outfit. DAVE COLLISTER

Approaching the island on the packed-out 14.15pm sailing from Heysham. Rain clouds seen over the north of the Island wet the roads during the TT practice. AUTHOR

Chris Palmer (350cc Walmsley AJS 5) goes inside of Mervyn Stratford (250cc Greeves) at Castletown Corner in the first Billown race for single cylinder classics. STAN BASNETT

Sunday 27 May

Classics down South

Jamie O'Brien heads the pack at the start of the Post Classic Superbike/850cc Classic race. He leads Peter Rubatto (dark visor) and eventual winner Guy Martin, racing with Number 0 because of an entries mix-up. DAVE COLLISTER

The Billown Pre-TT Classic races have been a curtain-raiser for the TT festival since 1988.

The demanding 4.25-mile circuit that starts and finishes on the A5 Castletown by-pass has a rich history, having been used to stage July's Southern 100 national road races since 1955. Classic racing, predominantly for pre-1973 four-strokes and pre-1967 two-strokes, saw massive growth in the Eighties. A Classic TT held on the Mountain Course in 1984 proved to be a one-off, but the Southern 100 Race Committee stepped up to lay on racing for historic machines in the early part of TT fortnight. The older bikes, with their loud exhausts and diversity of engine types are popular with spectators and not just those old enough to recall these machines the first time round.

This year's meeting, sponsored by Blackford Financial Services, was re-arranged so that racing would not clash with the Centenary celebrations at St John's on Monday 28 May. Practice was on Friday and Saturday, while one race was run on Saturday and the other races on Sunday.

Local riders figured prominently. Foxdale's Rich Hawkins won

Saturday afternoon's sunny single-cylinder event on a Ducati, from Chris Palmer on an AJS 7R Walmsley replica. Cumbria-born Palmer, who lives only 100 metres off the course in Castletown, topped Sunday afternoon's 500cc Senior race. He was on sponsor Miles Robinson's Walmsley Manx replica; the same machine he used to win the 2006 Manx Grand Prix Senior Classic race.

The weather deteriorated during Sunday's racing. At first some parts of the course had rain while others were sunny, but by the time the sidecar event started the whole circuit was wet. Rutland's Nick Houghton was the winner, passengered by Paul Thomas on a torquey 900cc twin-cylinder NRE-powered outfit, after early leaders Eddy Wright and Martin Hull hit trouble with their 900cc Hillman Imp car engine-powered outfit. German Ralf Engelhardt, who passengered sidecar champion Klaus Enders to Seventies' TT wins, was runner-up on his 980cc Busch BMW, passengered by Winnfried Viecenz. Manx-based veteran driver Dick Hawes was third with Tim Dixon on a 750cc Busch BMW outfit, also in Enders' red and white colours.

Belgian Eric Genin MIDDLE put up an outstanding performance for a newcomer at Billown, taking fifth place in a hard-fought Senior race. His result was all the more creditable because he had crashed at Joey's Gate in Friday practice.

"I woke up in the helicopter, but was discharged from hospital and okay to race," he said via an interpreter. Eric (40) is an organiser of historic races on a public roads circuit at Jehonville in the Ardennes region of Belgium. His Billown bike was a Matchless G50 owned by John Oldfield from Surrey RIGHT whose wife Julie is on the left.

There was oil on the road, as well as rain puddles, for the Quinn Kneale-sponsored 350cc Junior race. It was won by Blackpool's 2006 Manx GP Classic Lightweight victor Roy Richardson aboard a Honda CB350 twin owned by Martin Bullock's Manx-based racing team. Derek Whalley, whose home is beside the TT Course at Cronk-ny-Mona, was second on an Aermacchi single prepared by Dick Linton of FCL Racing.

Sunday evening's finale, the 4 Hire-sponsored combined Post-Classic Superbike/ 850cc Classic event was won convincingly by one of the modern TT favourites, Guy Martin. He was on John Sims' 750cc three-cylinder Triumph Trident, first raced at the Billown Pre-TT meeting by Alex George in 1992. Martin began by stalking Palmer on the 500cc Walmsley Manx single in tricky wet and, in places, oily conditions but then took the lead and extended it as the weather improved to head Palmer by more than 30 seconds at the flag. He set the fastest lap of the meeting at 89.338mph.

The third finisher and first home in the Post-Classic class was Billown newcomer Peter Rubatto from Germany, who finished fourth in the Formula 1 race in his first TT back in 1985. He was excluded from the results as he had entered the race for pre-1976 machines on a 1986 Yamaha-engined Bimota, purely through a misunderstanding. It was the same machine that he rode in the 1987 TT.

O'Brien using all of the road – and more – aboard his Yamaha on the exit from Ballakeighan Corner in the Post Classic race. The Liverpudlian really did overdo it moments later at Ballabeg and fell off. DAVE COLLISTER

Blackfords *Pre-TT Classic Races – Results*

Saturday 26 May
250cc-350cc Single Cylinder
1 Rich Hawkins   350 Ducati MkIII
2 Chris Palmer   350 AJS
3 Paul Dobbs   350 Aermacchi
FASTEST LAP RICH HAWKINS 84.242MPH

Sunday 27 May
250cc Lightweight
1 Geoff McMullen   250 Suzuki
2 Bill Wark   250 Suzuki
3 Terry Kermode   250 Yamaha
FASTEST LAP TERRY KERMODE 82.477MPH

500cc Senior
1 Chris Palmer   500 Norton
2 Roy Richardson   496 Bullock Honda
3 Alan Oversby   500 Craven Norton
FASTEST LAP CHRIS PALMER 88.645MPH

Sidecar
1 Nick Houghton/Paul Thomas   900 Nourish Windle
2 Ralf Engelhardt/Winnfried Viecenz   980 Busch BMW
3 Dick Hawes/Tim Dixon   745 Busch BMW
FASTEST LAP NICK HOUGHTON/PAUL THOMAS 75.793MPH

350cc Junior
1 Roy Richardson   349 Bullock Honda
2 Derek Whalley   349 FCL Aermacchi
3 Paul Coward   348 Fenna Honda
FASTEST LAP ROY RICHARDSON 83.002MPH

Post Classic Superbike
1 Guy Martin   750 Triumph Trident
2 Chris Palmer   500 Norton
3 Alan Oversby   500 Craven Norton
FASTEST LAP GUY MARTIN 89.338MPH

Mixed Class Support Race
1 John Jones   496 Seeley Matchless G50
2 Les Trotter   500 Suzuki
3 Keith McKay   981 Laverda Jota
FASTEST LAP LES TROTTER 77.665MPH

A rare opportunity to see the whole range of TT Trophies when they were put on show for the day on the stage of the Gaiety Theatre in Douglas. DAVE COLLISTER

TT legend Geoff Duke LEFT and chief marshal Roger Hurst at the official opening of premises for the TT Marshals Association behind the Grandstand. DOUBLE RED

Bad girls at Bushy's

Twisted Angels, a young Isle of Man-based four-piece all-girl band, played a frenzied gig in Bushy's beer tent on Douglas Promenade, launching two weeks of live music at the venue. DAVE COLLISTER

Alex Downie   Peter Dawson   Mick Grant   Sammy Miller   John Walker   Robert Lusk   Mike Jackson   Terence Wilson

1907 and all that:

St John's Circuit

- Kirk Michael — 7
- Glen Wyllin — 8
- 6
- Devil's Elbow — 9 — Barregarrow
- 10 — 5
- 4
- St Germain's — 11 — Cronk-y-Voddy
- Knocksharry
- 3 — Creg Willey's Hill
- Peel — 13 — 12
- 2 — Glen Helen
- Laurel Bank
- 14 — 1 — Ballig Bridge
- 15
- St John's — S — Ballacraine
- Start and finish

the re-enactment

One hundred years to the day after the first Tourist Trophy motorcycle race on 28 May 1907, big crowds gathered at the original start line in St John's to see ancient machines stage a glorious re-enactment on Bank Holiday Monday.

Jim Blanchard   Sir Paul Haddacks   Wyndham Rees   Anthony Stockman   Chris Read   Joyce Plant   Alan Bridge-Butler   George Cohen

Monday 28 May

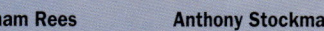
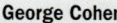

Start of the 1907 Tourist Trophy. FOTTOFINDERS

Geoff Duke unveiled a commemorative plaque. DAVE COLLISTER

Two 1907 machines start the Centenary 'race', watched by TT stars Ian Hutchinson and John McGuinness, seated by starter Geoff Duke's rostrum. DAVE COLLISTER

"Really good fun! I think we should do this every year," Mick Grant, winner of seven TTs 1974-1985.

The village green beside historic Tynwald Hill was a mass of colour as riders, officials and onlookers gathered for the 'race', many in authentic period clothing. Other points around the old 15.8-mile TT Course used from 1907 to 1910 were packed with spectators and despite ominous forecasts there was bright sunshine, appropriately accompanied by the chilly breeze mentioned in 1907 race reports.

Shortly before 11am, TT legend Geoff Duke dropped the Manx flag to start the 100th anniversary 'race'. The planned 10am start, which would have marked the centenary to the exact minute, had to be delayed for almost an hour while cars thoughtlessly parked on the course, mainly in the streets of Peel, were removed. As a result, the event was cut from two laps to one, probably a wise move anyway in view of the frailty of some of the machines.

Patrick McAloran   Ann Moore   Brian Draper   Robert Lusk   Chris Lewis   Tony East   Ivan Rhodes   Rupert Murden

The village of St John's is little changed since 1907, although they didn't have bouncy castles then, of course. AUTHOR

Dot Tilbury of IoM Post had the 1907 TT programme re-printed.
LILY PUBLICATIONS

Crazy! Dave MacMahon poses on his rorty 1912 Rudge Whitworth.
DAVE COLLISTER

The first two machines set off to follow the original TT Course, put-put-putting towards Ballacraine. Number One was the Peugeot-engined Norton believed to be the one on which Harry Rembrandt Fowler won the 1907 multi-cylinder race and set the fastest lap at 42.91mph. It was ridden by George Cohen, who restored this bike to running order for its owner, the National Motorcycle Museum in Birmingham.

Setting off alongside at Number Two was Chris Read on the Vindec Special thought to be the very machine on which American-born Billy Wells finished second to Fowler's Norton. Chris had contacted the IoM government offering to demonstrate his 1907 machine back in 2005.

An extraordinary array of well-preserved early machinery followed, starting two-by-two at one-minute intervals as they had in the first TT. Bride resident David Plant, who supplied no fewer than eight bikes for the event, set off on a 1908 Triumph similar to the model on which Jack Marshall won the 1908 single cylinder TT. It was an important victory for Triumph, because in 1907 Marshall had been second to Charlie Collier on a Matchless fitted with pedals to help him accelerate out of corners and climb the hills, such as the steep Creg Willeys ascent from Glen Helen to Lambfell. Since the TT's objective was to speed development of touring motorcycles, pedal assistance was decried by the Triumph factory and others, so pedals were banned for the 1908 race.

Waiting for the flag to drop. The startline official in Edwardian garb is Tony East, owner of the ARE Collection in Kirk Michael and one of the prime movers behind the successful event.
LILY PUBLICATIONS

| Author | Nick Jefferies | Ann Davy | Miles Cowsill | Milky Quayle | Mercury | Paul Phillips | Keith Jones |

Former TT racer and trials supremo Sammy Miller was on a 340cc Humber V-twin, thought to be Percy Evans's 1911 Junior TT-winning Humber. One of the 300 exhibits at Miller's Hampshire museum, the chuffing V-twin gleamed fresh from a total restoration last winter.

A much noisier take-off was made by Rudge specialist Dave McMahon on his roaring single-speeder, similar to the singles that were second in the 1913 Senior and victorious in 1914 for Rudge Whitworth of Coventry. Looking the part in his frog-eye period goggles and crash hat, Dave was a favourite with press photographers mobbing the start line.

Bearded Pat Davy, a stalwart of the organising Vintage Motor Cycle Club who has visited the Island every year since 1963, looked the part as he set off on the oldest surviving Dot. The marque's slogan was 'Devoid of Trouble', but Pat had spent the morning deep inside his ignition magneto, fortunately to good effect. His wife Ann rode a 1927 250cc Levis, a two-stroke of the type that dominated the earliest Lightweight TT races.

Flashback to colonial times as His Excellency the Governor arrives in a vintage Rolls-Royce. The car behind it is a rare 1913 Albion. DAVE COLLISTER

Anthony Edwards forges along on a 1932 Norton. The marque dominated the TT for much of the Thirties. DOUBLE RED

Current TT star Guy Martin adjusts his old-style helmet ready for the off on a Triumph Tiger 100. DOUBLE RED

The progressive Italian Moto Guzzi factory, which made its sensational TT debut in 1926 was represented by a Sport 14 flat single of the same period, ridden by Alex Downie MLC of the Isle of Man Treasury. His Guzzi jumper was just like that worn by Italian team riders in the Twenties.

Velocette historian Ivan Rhodes was on a very famous example of the marque, the 350cc works bike on which Alec Bennett won the 1928 Junior. He was definitely one of the fastest riders.

The 1907 start line was recreated by this ingenious method. DOUBLE RED

Geoff Hanson changes up as he sets off on a Sunbeam like the 1922 TT winner. LILY PUBLICATIONS

"That was a great ride. The bike went well, especially when I discovered on the Cronk-y-Voddy straight that it had a fourth gear!" Guy Martin.

Trevor Blunt on a 1913 Bradbury. It was restored to running order after being dragged from a river. DOUBLE RED

A bunch of Twenties' machines nearing the finish. Number 57 is Ivan Rhodes on Alec Bennett's 1928 Junior TT winner. DOUBLE RED

David Richards, 1909 Triumph TT Replica. DAVE COLLISTER

Nick Jefferies, winner of the 1976 Manx Two Day Trial, the 1983 Senior Manx Grand Prix and the 1993 Formula 1 TT, was togged up in a leather coat and flying helmet aboard a Scott Squirrel made in his home town of Shipley, West Yorkshire. Scott had early TT successes, winning the Senior in 1912 and 1913 with liquid-cooled two-stroke twins – precursors of the Yamaha TZs that came sixty years later.

Mick Grant, winner of seven TTs between 1974 and 1985, rode a 1938 Triumph Speed Twin from the ARE Collection based in Kirk Michael and managed to keep an (unlit) cigarette clamped between his lips for the whole lap. Other ARE vintage road bikes, kept in good order by their enthusiastic owner Tony East, were lent to 'celebrity' riders. Famous motorcycling writer Alan Cathcart cantered around on an Ariel Red Hunter single and current TT star Guy Martin had the loan of a pre-war Triumph, as well as an appropriate pudding basin helmet.

Soon getting used to the old-style right-foot gearchange, Guy zoomed his way to the front of the field, but officials flagged him down near the end of the lap to ensure that George Cohen on Number 1, who was travelling at a respectable speed himself, could take the chequered flag first.

OPPOSITE PAGE
Using all of the road on the Kirk Michael to Peel coastal section.
DAVE COLLISTER

Allan Simpson on Church Street in Peel. His 1908 Ariel single has been preserved by the Ariel owners Club. DAVE COLLISTER

Juris Ramba from Latvia was at St John's in period gear, but not riding in the re-enactment. He had arrived overnight and ridden his 1913 Rex belt-drive sidecar outfit from the Sea Terminal to his lodgings in Foxdale.

"Because the sidecar was full of luggage and tools the old bike could not make it up the hills and I had to get off and push," he explained. "I arrived just as the first cock was crowing, just before 4am. Later I was in pain so I went to hospital and they threatened to operate, but in the end they let me out. Maybe I will take the sidecar off the bike for the rest of the fortnight."

A group from the Seattle-based Vintage Motorcycle Enthusiasts at St John's. LEFT TO RIGHT Dick Casey, Pat Laughland, Jody Heintzman, Bill Maxwell, John Blanco and Richard Campbell. The VME organise an annual event called the Isle of Vashon TT on an Island in their area. LILY PUBLICATIONS

Nervous before the start, George was ecstatic at as he crossed the finish line, punching the air and shouting as the crowd cheered and clapped.

"The bike ran really well: it just flew up Creg Willey's Hill and felt as though it could easily have done another lap," George said, before calling the National Motorcycle Museum to confirm that its priceless Norton was still intact and running sweetly.

As the 100 participants came back from their ride and parked up their machines for the milling crowds to admire, they were bubbling with excitement. They all remarked on how enthusiastic the large crowds around

the course had been and some reported hairy moments. Nick Jefferies said he'd nearly been caught out by how sharp Ballacraine corner is when taken as a left-hander and 1909 Triumph rider David Richards reported taking a very wide line for the left turn at Kirk Michael. "These things just don't want to go round corners," he laughed.

The riders, officials and guests made for the refreshment tent, while a jazz band played and kids cavorted on a bouncy castle. It was a great day out and a fittingly festive celebration of the TT Centenary.

Yes! A triumphant George Cohen crosses the finish line on the 1907 ex-Rem Fowler Norton he restored for the National Motorcycle Museum. LILY PUBLICATIONS

Chequered flag, chequered bike. TT Riders' Liaison Officer Richard 'Milky' Quayle completes a lap on his replica of the Shuttleworth Snap seen in the 1936 George Formby film *No Limit*. DOUBLE RED

First timed practice

Carl Rennie rounds the Gooseneck on his Supersport with John McGuinness and Dan Stewart close behind. **DOUBLE RED**

The start of the first timed practice was delayed by 15 minutes until 6.30pm, while the Mountain Road was cleared after a road traffic incident. John McGuinness set the fastest lap of the session at 124.983mph.

Riders reported rain falling in various places.

"I realised it was damp when I nearly lost the front end at Pinfold Cottage," top-ranking IoM rider Paul Hunt said, still looking shaken when he arrived at the pits.

It was enough to make some pack up for the evening. But not McGuinness who, after riding his HM Plant Honda Superbike and Superstock machines, took out his Supersport Honda provided by racing dealer Padgetts.

"That's John, a real professional," team boss Clive Padgett commented.

The transponder-operated speed trap set up by Unysis at the eastern end of Sulby Straight showed McGuinness's HM Plant Honda team mate Ian Hutchinson fastest of the evening at 192mph. Pretty speedy, but not quite the 200mph that Superbikes were reputedly reaching at this point last year.

Bruce Anstey, winner of the 2005 and 2006 Superstock races was the fastest lapper in that class at 121.350mph on his Relentless by TAS Suzuki GSX-R1000. The 600cc Supersports

were topped by up-and-coming Manx rider Conor Cummins, best 2006 newcomer. It was a great way for him to celebrate his 21st birthday.

Michael Rutter, returning to the TT after a seven-year absence to ride for the Discovery Channel-sponsored MSS Kawasaki team said the roads felt smoother than he remembered them: "I think that's more to do with suspension improvements than the surface," the 1998 Junior race winner explained. His mechanics had taped a block of foam to the back of his bike's tank, to help take weight off a wrist injured earlier in the season.

New Zealander Shaun Harris, winner of both 2003 Production races, was another returnee getting back in the groove. "I feel like I'm home again – so relaxed I can't believe it," he said.

Riding in his second TT, 2005 Junior Manx GP winner Ian Pattinson was in the upper reaches of the times tables, being the fourth fastest Supersport and fifth best Superstock. The Weardale rider has ridden for Island-based Martin Bullock Racing, biggest of the independent teams, for several seasons.

For the second session running, Waterworks was the scene of an incident when Marc Ramsbotham, a newcomer from Norfolk, fell off while Yorkshire's Ian Armstrong who happily

Qualifying

Newcomers had to do six practice laps (Sidecars four laps) to qualify. Riders with TT or Manx GP experience needed five practice laps (Sidecars three), with a minimum of two on each machine entered, one of which must be inside qualifying time. Riders must complete a number of laps at a minimum speed to qualify.

Qualifying times:

Superbike and Senior	20m 30s	(110.43mph)
Superstock and Supersport	21m	(107.80mph)
Sidecar	24m	(94.32mph)

Experienced TT rider Ian Lougher glances across at spectators on the exit to the Gooseneck. DOUBLE RED

Getting to grips with factory tackle. Ian Hutchinson sweeps his HM Plant Honda CBR600 into Kirk Michael. DAVE COLLISTER

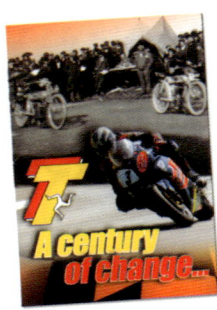

Italian, obviously. A limited-edition 650cc CRS Vun single displayed at the Paton camp. TRACEY HARDING

Failing light on the Mountain climb. DAVE COLLISTER

HM Plant Honda HQ. DOUBLE RED

Setting up Ian Lougher's 600cc Black Horse Honda Supersport. TRACEY HARDING

Fastest *laps*

Superbike TT

1	John McGuinness	HM Plant Honda	18m 06.77s	124.983mph
2	Ian Hutchinson	HM Plant Honda	18m 19.31s	123.558mph
3	Martin Finnegan	Alpha Boilers Honda	18m 32.27s	122.118mph
4	Ian Lougher	Stobart Honda	18m 40.25s	121.248mph
5	Adrian Archibald	TAS Suzuki	18m 42.74s	120.979mph
6	Ryan Farquhar	Mark Johns Honda	18m 47.06s	120.516mph

Superstock TT

1	Bruce Anstey	TAS Suzuki	18m 39.31s	121.350mph
2	Guy Martin	Hydrex Honda	19m 00.31s	119.115mph
3	Paul Hunt	Peter Beale Yamaha	19m 00.36s	119.109mph
4	Ryan Farquhar	Harker Kawasaki	19m 09.29s	118.184mph
5	Ian Pattinson	MBR Suzuki	19m 10.77s	118.032mph
6	Mark Parrett	C & C Yamaha	19m 18.44s	117.251mph

Supersport Junior TT

1	Conor Cummins	Millsport Yamaha	18m 51.40s	120.053mph
2	Chris Palmer	Solway Honda	19m 01.70s	118.970mph
3	Ian Lougher	Black Horse Honda	19m 14.86s	117.615mph
4	Ian Pattinson	MBR Honda	19m 22.32s	116.860mph
5	Nigel Beattie	Millsport Yamaha	19m 25.48s	116.543mph
6	Dan Stewart	Wilcock Yamaha	19m 30.45s	116.048mph

Sidecar TT

1	Nick Crowe/Dan Sayle	AJ Groundworks Honda	19m 51.60s	113.988mph
2	John Holden/Andrew Winkle	Suzuki	20m 29.11s	110.509mph
3	Klaus Klaffenbock/Christian Parzer	Alpha Boilers Honda	20m 40.63s	109.483mph
4	Allan Schofield/Peter Founds	Suzuki	21m 05.33s	107.346mph
5	Tony Elmer/Darren Marshall	Yamaha	21m 09.22s	107.017mph
6	Conrad Harrison/Kerry Williams	Honda	21m 21.97s	105.953mph

TT newcomer Steve Plater (in orange jacket) crests a bump alongside Manx hope Nigel Beattie on the approach to Kirk Michael.
DAVE COLLISTER

rides with 'unlucky' Number 13, spilled at Laurel bank. Neither was badly injured.

When Guy Martin toppled off at Governor's Bridge, caught out by his Hydrax Honda's minimal steering lock at walking pace, he parked the bike and lay on the grass on the inside of the hairpin while the Sidecars practised.

Roy Hanks, a Sidecar TT competitor since the Sixties, shepherded out some three-wheeled newcomers who had not made Saturday's practice. The weather was improving by then and the local pairing of Nick Crowe and Dan Sayle took their new Swiss-made LCR (Louis Christian Racing) chassis round at close to 114mph. Molyneux only managed 105mph, with an engine he had borrowed from a standard CBR600 at Tommy Leonard's Honda shop in Douglas while his race motor was being repaired. Japanese newcomers Masahito Watanabe and Hideyuki Yoshida completed two laps on their immaculate red and white LCR outfit powered by a 2006 Honda CBR600 engine.

Watanabe, who speaks little English commented: "Very bumpy!".

Belgian endurance racing specialist Michael Weynand nearly loses it at the Gooseneck. DOUBLE RED

TT Superbike

Fastest rider of the evening John McGuinness swoops through the double bend at Greeba Castle on his HM Plant Honda Superbike. DAVE COLLISTER

Steve Linsdell at Union Mills on the only two-stroke in the TT, a 500cc grand prix Paton that scored points in the 2001 world championships. DAVE COLLISTER

McGuinness set a scorching pace in Tuesday's solos practice, lapping at 128.492mph on his Honda Fireblade Superbike. He bettered the record he'd set himself in last year's TT Superbike, but not his outright record of 129.451mph set the in 2006 Senior. To be official, TT lap records must be set during a race.

For the Suzuki opposition, Bruce Anstey headed both the Superstock and Supersport classes on his Relentless by TAS machines, his best lap on the bigger bike being at more than 125mph.

Although conditions were bright and clear at the start of the session, it gradually turned dull and there were sprinkles of rain around the course. Nevertheless the paddock was busy: 175 solo machines and 68 sidecar outfits passed through the scrutineering bays. The Grandstand was bustling, too, with race day-sized crowds.

Two-stroke enthusiasts saw the only machine in this year's races with that type of engine complete two laps. The four-cylinder Paton PG500 built for the 2000 Grand Prix series was being ridden by TT regular Steve Linsdell for Milanese constructor Roberto Pattoni and his friend Giovanni Cabassi. The bike had died on Lambfell when the ignition rotor broke on Monday evening but Linsdell's Island-based backer Paul Mercer saved the day by machining a replacement.

"It's tricky to ride, because of the narrow power band. But when it comes on song it's as though the video has been put on fast-forward!" Linsdell said.

record tumbles

Photographers capture airborne action at the Ballaugh Bridge jump. LILY PUBLICATIONS

Avoid the rush

A new format for starting practice was tried for Tuesday's session, which proved a success. At the suggestion of some of the bigger teams, the faster riders with numbers from 1 to 30 were allowed to take their bikes onto Glencrutchery Road as soon as it was closed to traffic. As a result the chaotic rush to get onto the road through a narrow gate at the start of practice was avoided.

Conor Cummins had started the session on his Millsport Yamaha Superbike but parked it at his home town of Ramsey when the steering damper broke, begged a lift back to Douglas on the coast road and tore off again on his Superstock machine. He was then involved in a collision with experienced TT rider Alan Chamley at Laurel Bank. The Kendal rider lost control and came off to suffer concussion and minor fractures, while Cummins stopped to offer assistance at the scene and recover from the shock. Chamley, who spent several days in Nobles Hospital, blamed the incident on the Manx rider.

Waterworks (so called because it overlooks Ballure reservoir) claimed two more victims but fortunately neither came to much harm. They were William Dunlop, son of five-times TT winner Robert Dunlop and nephew of the late TT legend Joey Dunlop and Irish newcomer Roger Maher.

The Crowe and Sayle Sidecar team continued to show their outstanding class among the Sidecars. A lap at 114mph – their best ever – put them more than 5mph ahead of their nearest rivals in the session, Allan Schofield and Peter 'Dessy' Founds on their Suzuki-powered outfit. Dave Molyneux had worked mightily to get a hot engine back in his outfit but a fat lot of good it did him, as it broke down with a failed electronic cam lobe sensor after barely reaching the top of Bray Hill. A frustrated Moly called Tuesday 'my day from hell'.

Going full kilt

Wearing their 'Norfolk tartan' kilts, the Reepham Raptors were out in force at the Railway Inn for the practice. Pictured are FROM LEFT Baz, Vickers, Scrappydoo, Yoda and Dougal. "We don't wear kilts when we ride over the Mountain," Vickers explained. The genial group from Reepham, north of Norwich, were camping at nearby Glenlough.

Crowe *flies*

Fastest Sidecar crew Nick Crowe and Dan Sayle accelerate out of Greeba Bridge. Crowe was a double sidecar winner in 2006 after his mentor Dave Molyneux was sidelined by a practice smash. Fellow Manxman Sayle passengered Molyneux to his record-breaking 11th Sidecar win in 2005. Crowe's £35,000 outfit was only completed and tested a few weeks before practice started and its LCR chassis is a type that was tried by two competitors at the 2006 TT. Swiss engineer Louis Christian, who makes most of the chassis used in international sidecar grands prix, designed one conforming to the Formula 2 Sidecar rules applying at the TT.

After personally collecting the chassis from Switzerland, Nick filled it with a Honda CBR600 engine tuned by Chris Mehew in Lincolnshire and £5,000 worth of electronic kit. He acknowledged the backing he received from his sponsors, Andy Faragher of AJ Groundworks and Scott Shipping Management in Port St Mary. A dozen drivers raced the LCR F2 chassis this year, but none were more high-tech than Crowe's. **DAVE COLLISTER**

"The suspension is sorted but not the brakes" Nick Crowe

Fastest *laps*

Superbike TT

#	Rider	Machine	Time	Speed
1	John McGuinness	HM Plant Honda	17m 37.09s	128.492mph
2	Guy Martin	Hydrex Honda	17m 50.10s	126.931mph
3	Ian Lougher	Stobart Honda	17m 55.05s	126.346mph
4	Ian Hutchinson	HM Plant Honda	17m 55.70s	126.269mph
5	Martin Finnegan	Alpha Boilers Honda	18m 10.32s	124.576mph
6	Adrian Archibald	TAS Suzuki	18m 14.02s	124.155mph

Superstock TT

#	Rider	Machine	Time	Speed
1	Bruce Anstey	TAS Suzuki	18m 03.70s	125.338mph
2	Martin Finnegan	MV Agusta	18m 24.70s	122.954mph
3	Paul Hunt	Peter Beale Yamaha	18m 36.16s	121.692mph
4	Adrian Archibald	TAS Suzuki	18m 38.34s	121.456mph
5	Jamie McBride	Yamaha	18m 45.26s	120.708mph
6	John McGuinness	HM Plant Honda	18m 45.47s	120.686mph

Supersport Junior TT

#	Rider	Machine	Time	Speed
1	Bruce Anstey	TAS Suzuki	18m 39.47s	121.332mph
2	Ryan Farquhar	Harker Kawasaki	18m 47.72s	120.445mph
3	Ian Lougher	Black Horse Honda	18m 50.86s	120.110mph
4	Ian Hutchinson	HM Plant Honda	18m 52.17s	119.971mph
5	John McGuinness	Padgetts Honda	18m 52.19s	119.969mph
6	Shaun Harris	Blacks Suzuki	19m 07.27s	118.393mph

Sidecar TT

#	Crew	Machine	Time	Speed
1	Nick Crowe/Dan Sayle	600cc Honda	19m 49.32s	114.208mph
2	Allan Schofield/Peter Founds	600cc Suzuki	20m 48.10s	108.828mph
3	Simon Neary/Stuart Bond	600cc Yamaha	21m 02.11s	107.619mph
4	Steve Norbury/Scott Parnell	600cc Yamaha	21m 14.38s	106.584mph
5	Tony Elmer/Darren Marshall	600cc Yamaha	21m 18.06s	106.277mph
6	Andy Laidlow/Patrick Farrance	600cc Suzuki	21m 19.73s	106.138mph

A sunny scene on Glencrutchery Road by the Grandstand, where road bikers start and finish their laps of the Course on open roads. The roadway on the left is used by racers leaving the Course and returning to the paddock. LILY PUBLICATIONS

In conference

A three-day conference organised by Geoff Crowther of Huddersfield University Business School and Suzanne Ferris of Nova Southeastern Univesity, Florida was based at the Villa Marina. Called Heritage, Spirit and Place, it explored the historical, cultural and significance of the 100-year-old races and attracted delegates from as far afield as Japan, Canada and Russia.

A visit to the Manx Museum TT exhibition, a TT coach tour and spectating at practices were on the agenda, along with sessions discussing film, journalism and the role of motorcycle manufacturers.

Some of the many Australians at the TT: former sidecar racer Paul Robinson LEFT, his wife Veronica and friend shopping in Douglas. AUTHOR

Douglas Promenade began to liven up during practice week. BARRY EDWARDS

Bikers mix with busy normal traffic at Union Mills. LILY PUBLICATIONS

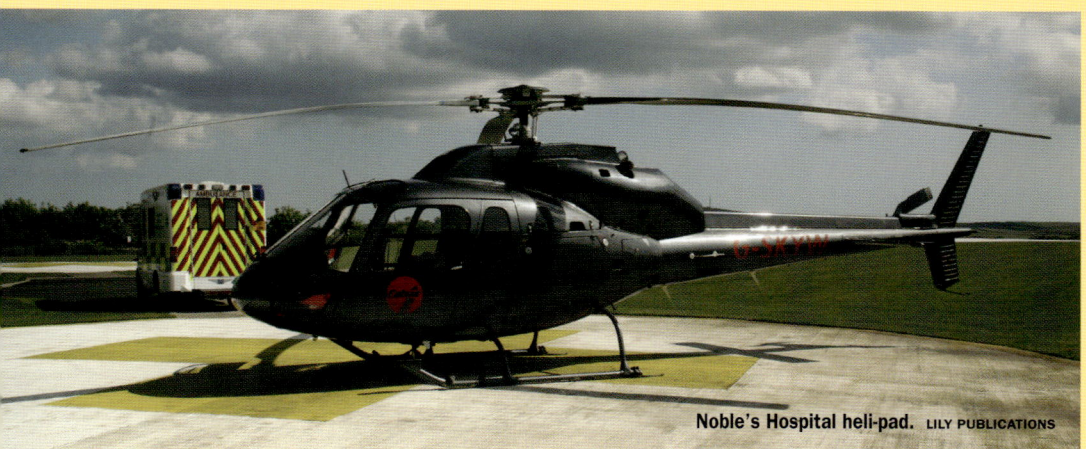

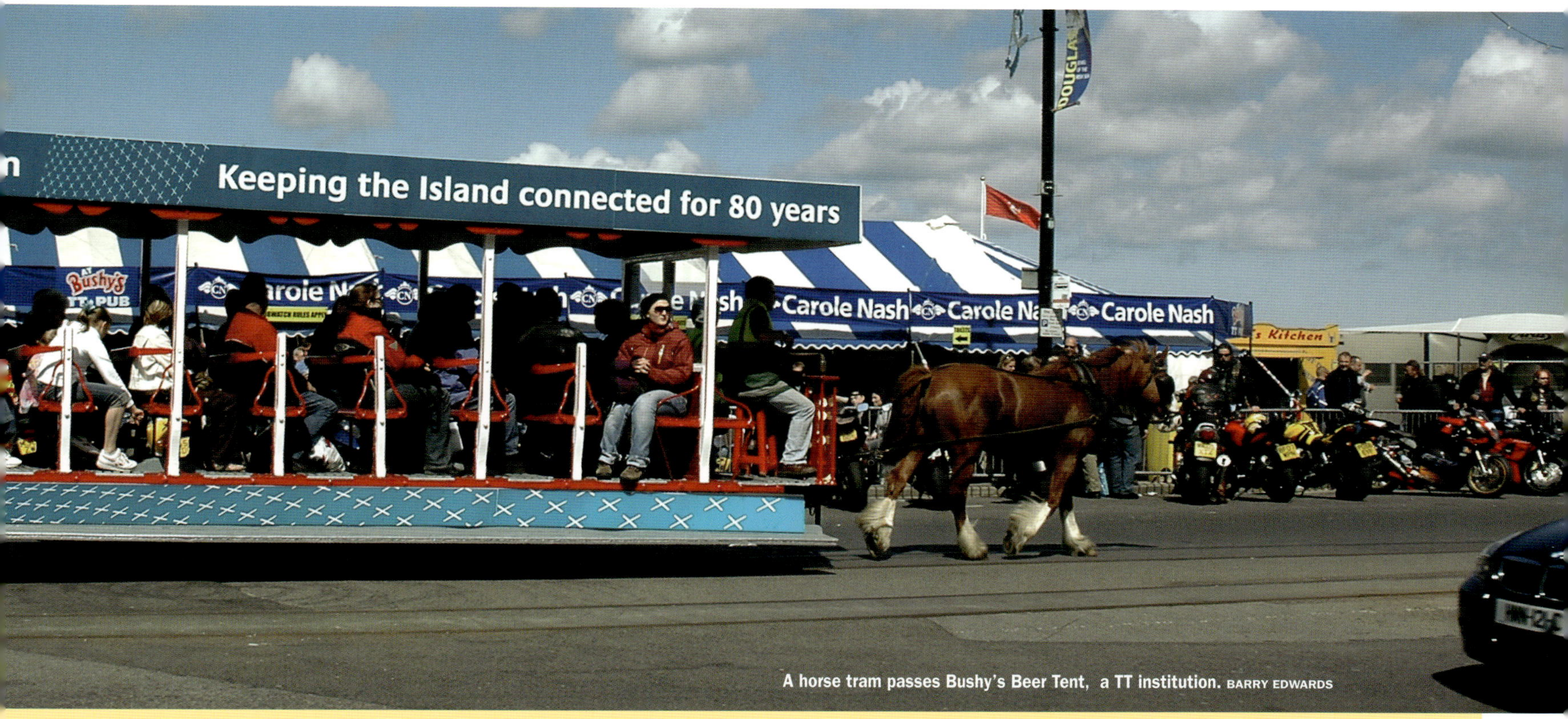
Keeping the Island connected for 80 years
Carole Nash
Carole Nash
Carole Nash
A horse tram passes Bushy's Beer Tent, a TT institution. BARRY EDWARDS

Helicopters stand by

Noble's Hospital heli-pad. LILY PUBLICATIONS

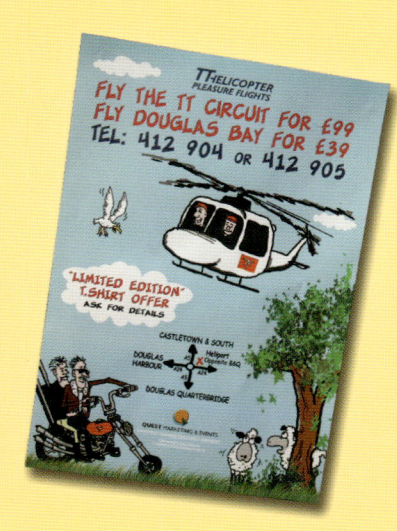

TT HELICOPTER
PLEASURE FLIGHTS
FLY THE TT CIRCUIT FOR £99
FLY DOUGLAS BAY FOR £39
TEL: 412 904 OR 412 905
"LIMITED EDITION"
T.SHIRT OFFER
ASK FOR DETAILS
CASTLETOWN & SOUTH
DOUGLAS HARBOUR
Heliport Opposite B&Q
DOUGLAS QUARTERBRIDGE

The sight-seeing helicopter at its base outside Douglas. IAN HARLAND

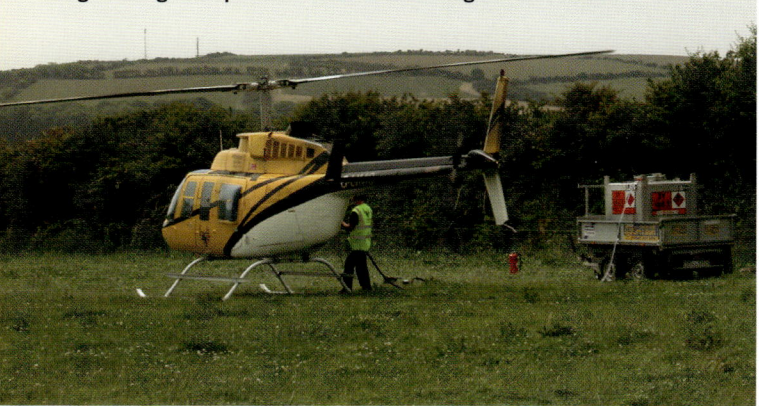

As has been usual in recent years, three helicopters were available to rush injured competitors to Noble's Hospital near Douglas. Two are hired specifically for TT work, while the third is brought in for the race period by the Island's health service. If low cloud or fog won't allow a helicopter to operate over the highest points of the Course, up to 427m (1400ft) above sea level, there is no racing regardless of conditions elsewhere.

Greenlight TV use a helicopter to film the racing and Quest marketing with Dragon Helicopters operate £99 pleasure trips around the Course at other times. To avoid queuing for aviation fuel at busy Ronaldsway Airport, Dragon had an approved storage tank made at short notice by specialist Metano Container on Tyneside and shipped overnight by Manx Hauliers ready for the Centenary TT.

Wednesday 30 May
Practice **cancelled**

Thick mist descending on the hills caused the practice to be cancelled. Even cloud hanging above the Course will stop a practice or race from being run if it that prevents the rescue helicopters from operating, but by Wednesday evening the fog was right down to road level, even below Creg-ny-Baa.

The missed session caused concern among some riders and teams, who were still trying to perfect suspension settings and finalise tyre choices, things that can only be done satisfactorily by turning in the laps.

PRF Racing Suzuki rider Carl Rennie, a 124mph-plus lapper in 2006, had been passed fit to race after breaking his collarbone in a crash at Ireland's Cookstown 100. But he decided to withdraw because he could not ride at competitive speed and returned to the mainland for an operation.

Traffic Report

The police reported 14 collisions on Manx roads during the week so far, fewer than in the same period in 2006. They said most accidents happened in built-up areas and involved overseas riders.

This is how the Course looked at Creg-ny-Baa by late afternoon. LILY PUBLICATIONS

"When we had the terrible first lap crashes in a 1978 Sidecar race, resulting in three fatalities, I was quoted as giving the TT five years. I'm pleased to say it proved otherwise. The TT has been a real survivor and here we are at the 100th anniversary." Geoff Cannell, veteran TT commentator and journalist on Radio TT Bikers' Breakfast programme.

Works MVs return

Factory technicians from the MV Agusta company arrived from Italy to make final adjustments to Martin Finnegan's Superstock machine, the marque's first officially-backed entry in the TT for 35 years.

The original MV company won 34 TTs between 1952 and 1972, but then withdrew on safety grounds at the request of 10-times winner Giacomo Agostini. At the end of 1976 the factory, predominantly involved with aviation, retired from the grand prix scene.

In 1992, the brand was acquired by Claudio and Gianfranco Castiglioni, at the time already owners of the Cagiva, Ducati, Morini and Husqvarna brands. Within five years they relaunched MV Agusta with the fanfare announcement of the superbly engineered upmarket 750cc four-cylinder F4.

A 1000cc version of the F4 followed in 2004 and when Finnegan's manager Barry Symmons (formerly with Honda Britain and John Player Norton) was seeking a Superstock for 2007 to augment Alpha Boilers Honda Superbike and Supersport rides, he sounded out MV via an Italian-speaking intermediary.

The response was enthusiastic and Symmons says that as soon as Martin tried the machine he thought it well suited to the Mountain Course with its bumps and jumps.

By Wednesday it was the second fastest Superstock after favourite Bruce Anstey's Suzuki GSX-R1000 and the team were quietly confident of a good showing.

Castletown Square, the destination for a Vintage Motor Cycle Club gathering, was bustling. LILY PUBLICATIONS

Gleaming on a dull day: a classic BSA Gold Star at the VMCC gathering. LILY PUBLICATIONS

Quiet outside, mayhem inside. A party of Swiss at the Jurby Airport Hotel enjoyed themselves, pirouetting their bikes to lay tyre 'doughnuts' on the bar-room floor. " They were a great bunch and no trouble at all. We managed to clean the floor up afterwards," said Aretha Lawson of the Hotel's staff. LILY PUBLICATIONS

Peel Bay Festival

The Who's lead guitarist Pete Townshend acknowledged that time spent on the Island in his childhood fostered his passion for music. ANDREW BARTON

No bigger act than The Who could have played the opening night of the Peel festival. The world-famous band, fronted by original Sixties' members Roger Daltrey and Pete Townshend, wowed the near-capacity 6,000-plus crowd with what everyone agreed was a storming performance.

Still in fine voice: the Who's lead singer Roger Daltrey. ANDREW BARTON

The support act was Back Door Slam, an acclaimed local band fresh from playing in the USA.

Thursday 31 May

Guy Martin brushes the bank at Keppel Gate on his Hydrex Honda Superbike, followed by Ian Lougher. Martin put in his best-ever lap at over 128mph. DAVE COLLISTER

'It's all very well people going on about dyno (engine power test) figures, but I've never yet seen anyone riding a dyno down Bray Hill' Guy Martin, during an paddock interview with Manx Radio's Chris Kinley.

Fast times were set during a session that started on time in fine weather. John McGuinness got up to race pace by reeling off a sizzling 129mph circuit on his Superbike, nudging his outright record. Another five Superbike contenders turned in sub-18 minute laps including Guy Martin, whose 17 minutes 39.78 seconds was his best yet.

Steve Plater showed that he was rapidly learning his way round by lapping superbly at more than 121mph, ranking him 16th fastest among the Superbikes. The next fastest newcomer in the class was 33 year old Scot Keith Amor, substituting for injured TT favourite Cameron Donald in Uel Duncan's Honda-backed team.

"I'm used to riding Superstocks and the Superbike is so different. It has so much power, it's a real animal and tries to wheelie everywhere. It has to be treated with respect," he said. "If I hadn't already ridden at the North West 200 and the Ulster GP, I'd never have been able to handle this course. I'm taking it steady and just letting the speed come gradually."

Multi-coloured insects, which inevitably accompany fine weather practice or racing on the island in June, were splattered on everyone's fairings and helmet visors.

When the Sidecars got their turn, an anxious Dave Molyneux was keen to get a couple of clean laps in.

Clerk of Course Neil Hanson and IoM Director of Motorsport Paul Phillips. LILY PUBLICATIONS

Dave Molyneux was eager to make progress after earlier troubles. Here, he and his seasoned new passenger Rick Long approach Rhencullen, where Moly had his outfit flip over and burn in the 2006 Thursday practice. DAVE COLLISTER

Crowds are rarely this big in practice week. Watching sidecars from the enclosure overlooking Braddan Bridge. LILY PUBLICATIONS

Re-acquaintance: Michael Rutter, last at the TT in 2000, passes Kate's Cottage on his MSS Discovery Kawasaki. DAVE COLLISTER

"The engine blow-up last weekend knocked us right back and put us way behind where we should be by now," he said. Steve Norbury, a Yorkshire driver with seven rostrum placings since 2003, was also worried because he had only completed one lap to date and needed at least one more to qualify. Veteran Roy Hanks also reported problems: "So far, we're getting through more engines than laps," he said. "I'm one of the drivers who switched from carburettors to fuel injection for this year and I haven't got the hang of the technology yet. I wish I'd got into computing a bit earlier in life – like when I was 50."

Manx rider Conor Cummins, who turned 21 in practice week, out of the seat on his JMF Millsport Yamaha at Rhencullen. He lapped at a shade under 123mph. DOUBLE RED

Two of the fastest local riders set off. Gary Carswell LEFT rides a Bolliger Team Kawasaki Superbike, Paul Hunt a Triumph Supersport sponsored by Cringle Construction. LILY PUBLICATIONS

"I use this bike to go to work on" Cheshire rider Mike Hose talking about the 2003 1000cc Aprilia V-twin he entered in the Superbike and Superstock races.

Fastest *laps*

Superbike
1	John McGuinness	HM Plant Honda	17m 32.24s	129.085mph
2	Guy Martin	Hydrex Honda	17m 39.78s	128.166mph
3	Ian Lougher	Stobart Honda	17m 40.00s	128.140mph
4	Ian Hutchinson	HM Plant Honda	17m 44.93s	127.546mph
5	Martin Finnegan	Alpha Boilers Honda	17m 47.06s	127.292mph
6	Bruce Anstey	TAS Suzuki	17m 54.07s	126.461mph

TT Superstock
1	Bruce Anstey	TAS Suzuki	18m 05.58s	125.120mph
2	John McGuinness	HM Plant Honda	18m 12.79s	124.295mph
3	Martin Finnegan	MV Agusta F4	18m 12.91s	124.281mph
4	Adrian Archibald	TAS Suzuki	18m 21.40s	123.323mph
5	Mark Parrett	C & C Yamaha	18m 27.78s	122.613mph
6	Guy Martin	Hydrex Honda	18m 29.89s	122.380mph

Supersport Junior TT
1	Bruce Anstey	TAS Suzuki	18m 27.72s	122.619mph
2	Guy Martin	Hydrex Honda	18m 31.26s	122.229mph
3	Ryan Farquhar	Harker Kawasaki	18m 32.80s	122.060mph
4	Ian Lougher	Black Horse	18m 42.89s	120.963mph
5	Michael Rutter	MSS Kawasaki	18m 47.82s	120.434mph
6	John McGuinness	Padgetts Honda	18m 49.63s	120.241mph

Sidcar TT
1	Nick Crowe/Dan Sayle	AJ Groundworks Honda	19m 50.17s	114.125mph
2	Dave Molyneux/Rick Long	HM Plant Honda	20m 14.12s	111.874mph
3	John Holden/Andrew Winkle	Suzuki	20m 30.07s	111.235mph
4	Allan Schofield/Peter Founds	Suzuki	20m 47.59s	108.872mph
5	Simon Neary/Stuart Bond	Yamaha	20m 47.61s	108.871mph
6	Steve Norbury /Scott Parnell	Lockside Yamaha	20m 50.80s	108.595mph

Guy Martin aims his Hydrex Honda down the hill to Creg-ny-Baa. DAVE COLLISTER

It was the first time in TT history that a Thursday practice was held in the evening. In the Thirties, when evening sessions were introduced to accompany the traditional early morning practices, an afternoon session was also established on what was then 'early closing day' for shops. In recent years, closing the roads at a time when they are extremely busy with day-to-today traffic has been considered undesirable and the Manx Grand Prix led the way by changing its Thursday practice from the afternoon to the normal evening slot .

The session start time was delayed by 25 minutes because all three rescue helicopters were occupied in dealing with a traffic accident at Greeba.

Consolation cash

The TT Riders Association announced that it would award a £100 cash prize to the highest finishing rider in each race not to gain a replica trophy (awarded for finishing within 110 per cent of the winner's time). "We thought it a better use for money than organising yet another function and we know riders struggling to get replicas can always use the cash," Frances Thorp, secretary of the TTRA said. The charitable organisation also provided bottles of a medically-approved energy drink to all competitors.

Proper racing

Newcomer Rob Barber was offered a TT ride after he said in a magazine interview that racing on the Isle of Man was his ambition. "This is proper racing and everyone helps each other – not like British Superbike," said Bob (27), who started riding aged six and was a member of the Great Britain team in the international Suzuki GSX-R Cup series.

THIS SESSION
ENDS AT
19 - 55

DJ Replica

A replica of the 2000 V&M Yamaha R1 ridden by the late TT legend David Jefferies, winner of nine TTs, was commissioned by his father Tony, a triple winner himself. It is being raffled in association with Motor Cycle News to raise funds for the David Jefferies memorial foundation. If you are reading this before October 2007, you could win it: see www.davidjefferiesracing.com or call 01733 887388. **MOTOR CYLE NEWS**

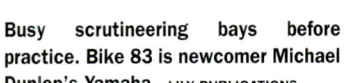

Busy scrutineering bays before practice. Bike 83 is newcomer Michael Dunlop's Yamaha. **LILY PUBLICATIONS**

Former TT winner Milky Quayle gave national press journalists pillion rides to promote the TT. The bike is a Suzuki TT Centenary edition GSX-R1000.
DOUBLE RED

Gull catcher

Local rider John Crellin completed almost half a lap with this unfortunate seagull jammed in the fairing. "It was standing on the road at Milntown and took off as I approached," John explained. "There was big bang and a flurry of feathers and I thought it had gone under the wheels. Everything seemed okay so I decided it was business as usual and carried on. I had almost forgotten about it until I came in to change bikes and everyone was staring and pointing at me."

The crowded paddock area before practising started in bright conditions.
LILY PUBLICATIONS

Wade in

WADE BOYD WAS PLEASED TO BE PRACTISING FOR THE TT SUPERSPORT RACE ON A HALLETT AVIATION KAWASAKI. THE POPULAR CALIFORNIAN HAS RACED IN THE LAST 14 TTs BUT HAD HIS ENTRY FOR 2007 REJECTED.

He raised a petition and appealed, but without success. Having already spent a considerable amount of money he travelled to the Island anyway and marshalled at early practice sessions. When some riders withdrew in practice week, Wade was permitted to take over Swede Martin Hamberg's number on a loaned bike.

Other riders gained late Supersport entries. One was Manx resident Kevin Murphy, known since his childhood in Dublin as the 'Irish Ago' because he used to wheelie his bicycle to emulate his hero Giacomo Agostini. He took over Argentinian David Paredes' Triumph entry on a Bill Smith Motors bike. Another was Phil Gilmore, who got a Yamaha ride.

Well baked. A TT Centenary cake produced by students from the Isle of Man College. Sold during the evening, it raised money for charities. LILY PUBLICATIONS

What a scorcher!

Things were hotting up on Douglas Promenade.

The Frying Dutchman? Deranged attention-seeker Michel Kooij from Holland gave the Pyromaniac Jet Quad its first fiery TT outing of 2007. DOUBLE RED

Re-formed Eighties' Scots band Deacon Blue topped the bill on the second night of the Festival. ANDREW BARTON

Peel Bay *Festival*

The other performers were music scene veteran Paul Carrick ABOVE and Steve Gibbons RIGHT a long-time favourite with TT crowds.
ANDREW BARTON

A hedge fire holds up practice

The tops of the hills were perfectly clear against a deep blue sky on Friday evening, offering the promise of a belting practice session. But as starting time approached a 15-minute delay was announced for the second evening running, this time due to a road accident at Greeba.

When the riders got away they were flying. Ian Hutchinson went through the Sulby speed trap at close to 187mph and John McGuinness clocked 165mph on his 600cc Supersport. But by the time the fastest men were completing their first lap, the session was being red-flagged.

Three riders had come off in the twisty Glen Helen section near the Black Dub. Belgian rider Michael Weynand had crashed heavily, and both Victor Gilmore and Jim Hodson had been unable to avoid the melée. A petrol tank burst into flames, setting fire to roadside vegetation and the practice was stopped so that a fire appliance from Peel could tackle the blaze before it spread. A road sweeping truck also attended the scene to clean up, a process that took half an hour out of the remaining practice time.

Bolliger Kawasaki teamster Weynand, an experienced endurance racer and a member of the 120mph-plus club, suffered lower leg injuries and Gilmour damaged a shoulder, while Hodson was uninjured. When the session eventually resumed, Hutchinson put in a flyer at over 127mph.

Friday 1 June

David Paredes practising on his Yamaha Superbike. Lack of funds forced him to withdraw from the Supersport TT. From Argentina, Paredes has competed since 2000, along with compatriot Walter Cordoba who did not get an entry this year. DOUBLE RED

Fastest Supersport of the session was the Padgetts Honda ridden by John McGuinness, not included in the HM Plant team for the 600cc race. Seen here on the Mountain, he lapped at 122.423mph. DOUBLE RED

Lapping at more than 124mph, Martin Finnegan served warning that the MV Agusta is a serious Superstock threat. DAVE COLLISTER

"I'm more nervous than I've ever been this year. I feel like I'm carrying ten bags of cement at the moment," John McGuinness talking at HM Plant's press reception after Friday's practice.

"We've been chipping away at it steadily," he said of his first TT practices with the HM Plant Honda team. "I've been getting used to the bikes and tyres and I've been surprised at how close to short circuit settings we've ended up. On the 600 Supersport you get time to look around you, but on the Superbike your head is wobbling around so much it's a job just to see where the kerbs are."

Kettering's James McBride, riding in his fifth TT, showed that he is rising through the ranks by placing fourth in the Superstock times on his Yamaha R1 with a lap at more than 121mph.

Paul Hunt and Ryan Farquhar had a close shave when they momentarily collided on the fast approach to Alpine Cottage. Both stayed in control, although local firefighter Hunt lost the brake lever from his right handlebar in the incident.

When the sidecars went out, Dan Clarke, desperate to qualify for racing, crashed at Bedstead Corner and was taken to hospital with fractures and detained. His passenger Nigel Mayers was discharged the next day.

Cushioning of immovable objects around the Course is constantly improved, but has to be arranged so as not to block footpaths or shop entrances. LILY PUBLICATIONS

John Holden, third in the 2006 Sidecar A race, pushed his Suzuki-powered LCR outfit to a personal best of 111.235mph. Here, he and ballast Andrew Winkle sweep through The Bungalow. DOUBLE RED

The cleanest and most checked public highway in the world? Marshals walk towards Cruickshanks Corner at the foot of May Hill in Ramsey on a closed road. STAN BASNETT

A fine evening for watching at The Bungalow. DOUBLE RED

"My 200 horsepower Superbike is a bit different round here from the wee thing I won a Manx Grand Prix on last year. That only had about 45." Michael Dunlop, winner of the 125cc/400cc Manx GP newcomers race in 2006.

Travelling Marshals returning to the Grandstand in fading light at the end of practice. DOUBLE RED

Fastest laps

TT Superbike

1	Ian Hutchinson	1000cc Honda	17m 49.10s	127.049mph
2	Bruce Anstey	1000cc Suzuki	17m 57.85s	126.017mph
3	Ryan Farquhar	1000cc Honda	18m 12.59s	124.317mph
4	Martin Finnegan	1000cc Honda	18m 13.57s	124.206mph
5	Adrian Archibald	1000cc Suzuki	18m 13.62s	124.201mph
6	Michael Rutter	1000cc Kawasaki	18m 14.38s	124.114mph

Junior TT

1	John McGuinness	600cc Honda CBR	18m 29.50s	122.423mph
2	Shaun Harris	600cc Suzuki GSX-R	18m 46.65s	120.560mph
3	Conor Cummins	600cc Yamaha YZF R6	19m 06.23s	118.500mph
4	Ian Pattinson	600cc Honda CBR	19m 08.03s	118.314mph
5	Michael Rutter	600cc Kawasaki ZX6R	19m 08.30s	118.286mph
6	Chris Heath	Yamaha YZF R6	19m 31.28s	115.965mph

TT Superstock

1	Ian Hutchinson	1000cc Honda Fireblade	18m 01.69s	125.570mph
2	Martin Finnegan	1000cc MV Agusta F4	18m 12.53s	124.325mph
3	Adrian Archibald	1000cc Suzuki GSX-R	18m 15.72s	123.963mph
4	James McBride	1000cc Yamaha R1	18m 34.22s	121.904mph
5	Paul Hunt	1000cc Yamaha R1	18m 41.08s	121.158mph
6	Nigel Beattie	1000cc Yamaha R1	18m 41.68s	121.094mph

Sidecar TT

1	Dave Molyneux/Rick Long	600cc Honda	20m 04.39s	112.778mph
2	John Holden/Andrew Winkle	600cc Suzuki	20m 21.09s	111.235mph
3	Steve Norbury/Scott Parnell	600cc Yamaha	20m 32.66s	110.191mph
4	Allan Schofield/Peter Founds	600cc Suzuki	20m 32.93s	110.167mph
5	Greg Lambert/Gary Partridge	600cc Honda	20m 51.80s	108.506mph
6	Nigel Connole/Jamie Winn	600cc Honda	20m 57.73s	107.995mph

Dazzling Dunlop display

An exhibition of trophies won by the late TT legend Joey Dunlop in his brilliant road racing career from 1969 to 2000, along with several sets of Joey's leathers, was held in the Promenade Suite at the Villa Marina. The dazzling display was made possible by Joey's widow Linda and it raised funds for the Joey Dunlop Foundation. More than £8,600 was taken in entrance fees and almost the same amount again from selling merchandise and tombola tickets.

There were many other collections for the fund during the fortnight and one race team alone, the Alpha Boilers/Klaffi equipe, collected more than £3,000.

The Joey Dunlop Foundation is building a five-unit holiday complex for disabled people on Victoria Road near the Grandstand, where priority will be given to ex-TT and Manx GP competitors.

Just part of the display at the Villa Marina. **FOTTOFINDERS**

Former Honda UK boss Bob McMillan presents one of Joey's helmets from his last racing season in 2000 to his widow Linda LEFT and daughter Donna. **AUTHOR**

Engine man

Tony 'Slick' Bass is one of the unsung heroes of the TT; an engine specialist who works all hours to service customers. Formerly a mechanic for Joey Dunlop, Carl Fogarty and other top riders, he moved to the Isle of Man five years ago and set up Slick Performance in workshops at Andreas. His engines have won five Sidecar TTs and this year he backed local rider John Barton and was a consultant to the MSS Discovery Kawasaki team.

"Sometimes I have 20 customers all wanting their engines done as soon as possible," said Tony, who charges roughly £1100, plus parts, to build a motor to full-race tune. **LILY PUBLICATIONS**

Troubled waters

The Isle of Man Steam Packet Company, the monopoly passenger ferry service connecting the Island with the UK and Ireland, came in for heavy criticism even before the TT festival got underway. Customers booking ahead had to pay deposits before being told what fares they would be charged. Some travellers from Australia and the USA were expected to make TT plans without knowing definite sailing times.

The company, which sold a car ferry in 2005, had a catamaran put out of service by a collision on the River Mersey in February. Extra passenger and freight ships were chartered for TT time, but arrangements were not finalized until a late stage.

Just prior to TT fortnight 5,000 customers were contacted, some at very short notice, and told that the times, and in some cases the departure ports, of their sailings had been altered. Some Continental visitors were badly affected: a German biker's revised timings gave him only 15 minutes to ride from Liverpool for his onward departure from Hull. The Steam Packet struggled to cope with concerned callers and websites carried scathing comments. Problems on 28 May were exacerbated by a failure of a loading ramp used by the company at the port of Heysham.

However, the beleaguered company and its hard-working staff did manage to carry nearly 50,000 passengers and an estimated 20,000 motorcycles on 400 sailings in and out of Douglas over the TT period.

Some senior Manx politicians strongly defended the Steam Packet's performance, but there is no doubt that there were a substantial number of dissatisfied customers this year and for many TT visitors the ferry service forms their first impression of the Isle of Man.

The Steam Packet ferry disgorges another full load of bikers. LILY PUBLICATIONS

How did they get the tent pegs in? Camping on the South Quay at Douglas. STAN BASNETT

IDEAL FOR RADIO TT AM - FM RADIOS COMPLETE WITH HEADPHONES, BUILT IN SPEAKER BELT CLIP
£9.95 INCLUDING BATTERIES

Honda displayed historic racing machines, including ex-Joey Dunlop bikes, in the atrium at the Sefton Hotel on Douglas Promenade.
TRACEY HARDING

Peel Bay *Festival*

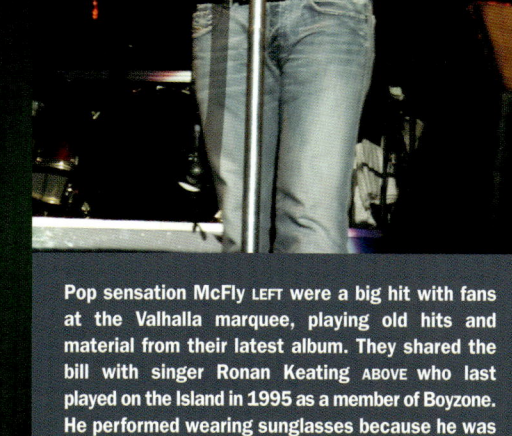

Pop sensation McFly LEFT were a big hit with fans at the Valhalla marquee, playing old hits and material from their latest album. They shared the bill with singer Ronan Keating ABOVE who last played on the Island in 1995 as a member of Boyzone. He performed wearing sunglasses because he was suffering from an eye infection. ANDREW BARTON

No racing *today*
Saturday 2 June

The morning Paddock Walkabout in the Grandstand area provided an opportunity for the public to meet the TT riders, get their autographs and watch team crews making final preparations for the Superbike race.

Cloudy skies suggested that the start of the first Centenary TT race, due to get under way at 12 noon, might be postponed.

RIGHT
John McGuinness signs for young fans. TRACEY HARDING

BELOW
Historic racers of the Yamaha Classic Racing Team on display in the paddock. BARRY EDWARDS

Although the pre-race procedures began on time, riders were warned of damp patches at several points around the Course. Then there was a half-hour delay because an oil spill on the road at The Bungalow had to be cleaned up. But it looked as though the race was definitely on, as riders and machines lined up on Glencrutchery Road – until a few minutes before the off, when it was announced that there would be no racing that day. Sudden deterioration of the weather on the Mountain was given as the reason.

The programme was to be re-arranged so that the postponed Superbike and Sidecar A races would run on Monday, while the Superstock race and Dunlop Lap of Honour scheduled for Monday would move to Tuesday.

It had been rumoured in the paddock before noon that some of the top riders were urging the organisers to postpone racing until Monday because the weather forecast

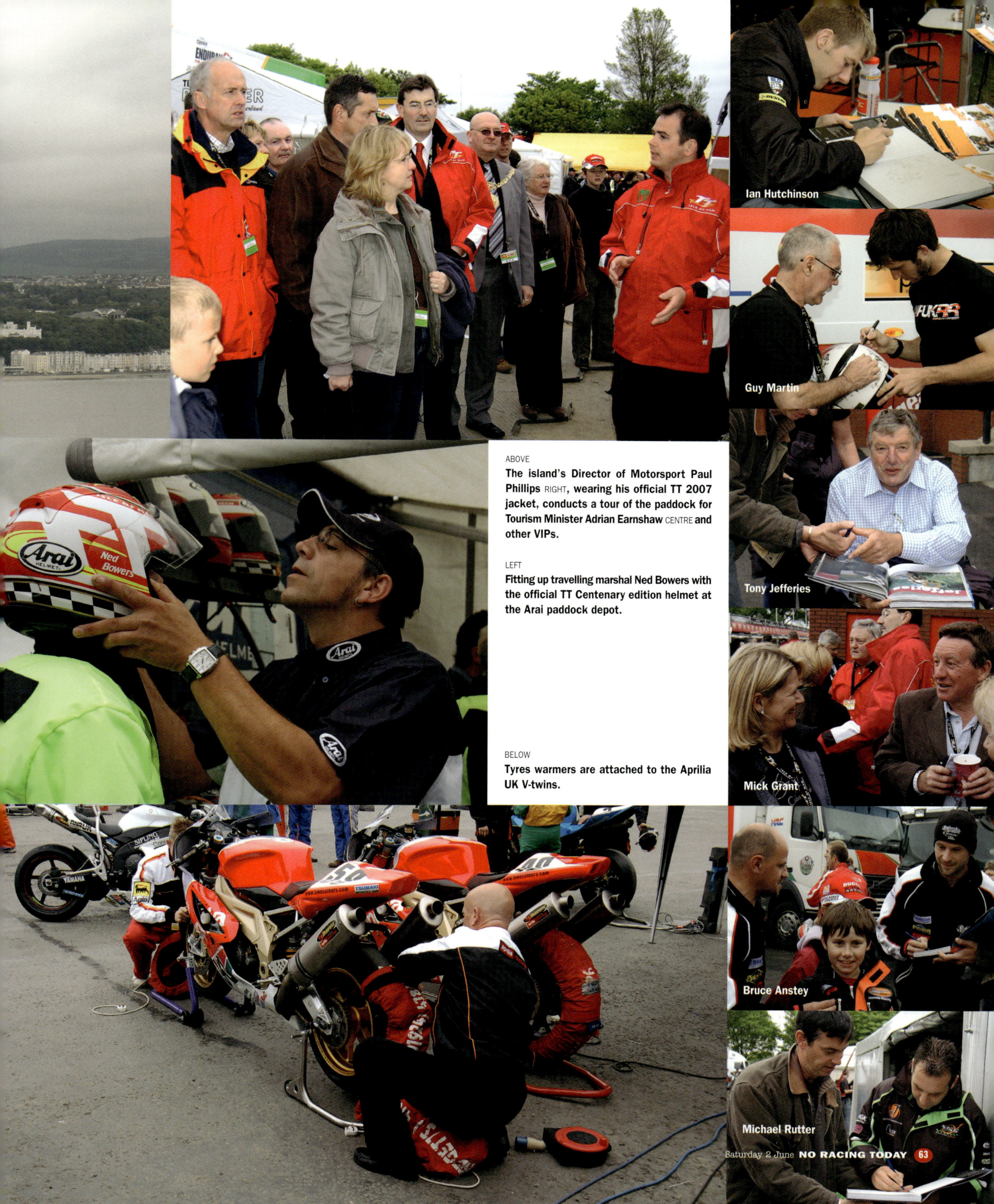

Ian Hutchinson

Guy Martin

Tony Jefferies

Mick Grant

ABOVE
The island's Director of Motorsport Paul Phillips RIGHT, wearing his official TT 2007 jacket, conducts a tour of the paddock for Tourism Minister Adrian Earnshaw CENTRE and other VIPs.

LEFT
Fitting up travelling marshal Ned Bowers with the official TT Centenary edition helmet at the Arai paddock depot.

BELOW
Tyres warmers are attached to the Aprilia UK V-twins.

Bruce Anstey

Michael Rutter

Contemplation. John McGuinness on the starting grid. DOUBLE RED

predicted fine and dry conditions by then. Their alleged argument was: why risk a race that might have to be shortened due to weather? It would disappoint the huge Centenary crowds, when racing on dry roads seemed assured for the week ahead.

In the event a few of the fastest riders who were contracted to ride on Dunlop tyres had reason to be relieved at the postponement. They had been waiting on the start line with untreaded slick tyres, obviously not suited to wet conditions.

Hand-cutting treads in the Dunlop truck: they were told it was illegal AUTHOR

Earlier Dunlop had recommended that their riders use intermediate tyres, actually slicks with treads cut on them by hand with a special tool. But not long before the race was due to run, the organisers confirmed that such tyres were prohibited by the regulations for the Superbike TT.

Unlike Pirelli, the other tyre supplier for solo TTs, Dunlop were not able to offer intermediates with moulded treads. 'Full wet' tyres wear out too quickly for TT racing.

Serious talk: Ian Hutchinson LEFT and Michael Rutter with riders' liaison officer Richard 'Milky' Quayle, before the two-day postponement was announced. DOUBLE RED

It's dry and clear on Glencrutchery Road, but what will it be like on the Mountain? DOUBLE RED

Steve Plater waits. DOUBLE RED

Trying to be relaxed. Guy Martin sits and waits. DOUBLE RED

Riders' crews clear the pits and drain the fuel fillers. DOUBLE RED

Dunlop chief Phil Plater had debated the issue with Deputy Clerk of the Course Eddie Nelson of the Auto Cycle Union and was told that 'cut slicks' were definitely not allowed and that the FIM (Federation Internationale Motorcyclisme, the ultimate racing authority) had a rule stating that tread patterns had to be as applied by the tyre maker during the manufacturing process.

"The regulations are issued to riders and teams but not to us in the trade," Phil Plater said. "It seems this rule first applied in 2006, but because of the dry weather it was not an issue. I would maintain that any tyre emerging from our truck is an official approved Dunlop manufactured product. We expect that cut tyres will be allowed in 2008."

Riders who had been ready and willing to race in the conditions as they were when the postponement was announced expressed frustration and visitors who had to return home before seeing any racing were naturally disappointed.

The weather remained cloudy and dull, but plenty of bikers used the re-scheduling to put in more brisk laps of the Course. The consensus was that the permanent one-way system on the Mountain was a good move, improving safety as well as offering riders the freedom to use the whole road for high-speed riding.

Not today. Bikes are wheeled off the starting grid. DOUBLE RED

Fun on the Prom

There may have been no racing, but there was plenty to see on Douglas Promenade where the third successive night of fun and games entertained a large and lively crowd.

John Reynolds shows off Suzuki's B-King. DOUBLE RED

Three-quarters of a mile of road from the sea terminal to the bottom of Broadway was closed to traffic and for the first time, the main arena for displays was at the northernmost end, adjacent to the Villa Marina. It was overlooked by two giant screens so that everyone could see all the action as it was filmed live by powerful cameras. At other times, the screens were used to play coverage of the TT races and footage from the past. A prime viewing area above the Villa Marina colonnade was reserved for ticket holders only.

The TT freestyle stunt championship went into its second night, with two rounds during the evening. An international line-up of five riders took part: Christian Pfeiffer (Germany), Humberto Ribeiro (Portugal), Matti Tepsa (Sweden), Mattie Griffin (Ireland) and Zoltan Angyal (Hungary).

The Island's own stunt rider, trials genius Steve Colley, did his amazing two-wheeled ballet nightly as well as being on the judges' panel for the stunt contest. Popular Mini-driving stunt man Russ Swift amazed and amused with his incredible high-speed parking act and another TT favourite, the Pyromaniac Jet Quad, came out before bedtime.

Suzuki sprang a surprise when three-times British Superbike champion John Reynolds demonstrated the company's exciting new 1300cc B-King ahead of its official UK release later in the year. The long-awaited muscle bike was first seen as a radically-styled concept bike at the 2001 Tokyo Show.

Smoking in a public place: the irrepressible Pyromaniac Jet Quad. DOUBLE RED

A refreshments area, including the TT Century Bar and various fast food concessions, linked the spectating area to the funfair that had been set up on the Loch Promenade since Wednesday.

At the Sea Terminal end of the Prom, another entertainment area with its own screen was overlooked by Bushy's Beer tent. Stunt riders Ashley Mark, Dave Coates and Neil Porter were on at various times and anyone could have a go at staying on the fiendish mechanical Rodeo Bull.

The Pirelli tyre company was on hand with a stack of part-worn rear tyres from the British Superbike series, which were fitted free to anyone performing a thorough burn-out for the crowd.

Manx Radio's AM station Radio TT had its outside base in this area at the Arai pitch.

The sensational Bolldogs freestyle team performed in the early evening. The stone column behind is the Douglas War Memorial. STAN BASNETT

Peel Bay
Festival

Police joined in the fun, but revellers ending up in court faced heavy penalties. **DAVE COLLISTER**

World-class extreme stunts from Christian Pfeiffer on a BMW F800. **DAVE COLLISTER**

Former BeeGee Robin Gibb topped the Peel Festival bill. The singer and writer, who with his brothers Barry and Maurice lived on the Isle of Man as a child, announced that he would waive his appearance fee with the money to go to the children's ward at the local hospital. Others playing Peel were powerful-voiced singer Bonnie Tyler and Chris Norman, formerly of Smokie, plus local groups Chiaroscura and Stone Creation. **ANDREW BARTON**

Chris Norman, formerly of Smokie and Bonnie Tyler **ANDREW BARTON**

A not so Mad Sunday

Sunday 3 June

3 MILESTONE

Not the day for a fast blast over the Mountain. Visibility was this bad down at Creg-ny-Baa, never mind the higher parts of the Course. TRACEY HARDING

Hailstones that turned the Mountain Road white first thing in the morning did not bode well and occasional rain fell in various parts of the Island during the day, setting in heavily for a time in the late afternoon. Those bikers who maintained the Mad Sunday tradition of thrashing round the Course were forced to take the Mountain Road slowly because visibility was severely limited. According to the police it was more like Sensible Sunday: "It has been quiet with few incidents and we hope it stays that way," a spokesman said at the end of the day.

The many events scheduled for the day went ahead regardless, from the bigger Honda, Suzuki and Yamaha promotions to several smaller one-make owners' gatherings. There were three TT Church services, a vintage tractor display, TT Teas in Bride Church Hall and Speedy Snacks at St Jude's old school near Sulby. To raise even the dampest spirits on a wet evening, the Purple Helmets staged their big show at Onchan Stadium.

Things didn't look much better in Douglas. TRACEY HARDING

The vintage crowd gather in Castletown Square. AUTHOR

The Centenary attracted a bumper entry of more than 200 machines built prior to 1982 for the annual Vintage Motor Cycle Club TT Rally. Several of them had been on the island for the 1907 TT Re-enactment, but the first full gathering was in the main square at Castletown on Mad Sunday.

Truly international, the rally was attended by 17 French enthusiasts who stayed at Sulby Church Hall, an American member and seven from Poland, two of whom were co-incidentally Mayors of their home towns.

It was raining as the old machines, many of them in gleaming restored condition, began to arrive but dried up for the concours competition to select the best-kept and most desirable bikes.

CASTLETOWN CONCOURS RESULTS

FOOTMAN JAMES CUP – BEST PRE-WAR UP TO 1940 1913 Rex JAP, owner Juris Ramba
BONHAMS ROSEBOWL – BEST POSTWAR 1941-1960 1951 Vincent Rapide, owner William Bewley
H & H CLASSIC AUCTIONS ROSEBOWL – BEST POSTWAR 1961-1982 1961 Norton Navigator, owner Terry Brock
BEST MACHINE MANUFACTURED OUTSIDE THE UK 1935 Harley-Davidson, owner Richard Brodziak

A spot of rain didn't trouble the hardy Hesketh Owners Club members assembled in Castletown Square for their TT gathering to celebrate the 25th anniversaries of both the British-made Hesketh V1000 motorcycle and the club. Merv Matthews won a cup for the best bike, judged for the club by Richard Ronan of Castletown Town Commissioners. AUTHOR

CASTLETOWN VMCC GATHERING

The Sidings pub next to Castletown railway station hosted a German brunch organised by TT rider Franz Spenner and former competitor Martin Grein at the suggestion of Heike Perry, Manx Radio's German language TT announcer. The event raised funds for air rescue on the nearby Billown racing circuit.

Markus and Kirsten Badstöber were in Castletown for the German brunch and to see the vintage bike gathering. "We like classic bikes and have eight Yamaha SR500 singles from the Seventies," Markus explained. "We've seen old bikes being ridden over here that we'd just never see in Germany. The couple from the Stuttgart area usually attend the Manx GP to watch classic racing, but decided that they should be at the Centenary TT. AUTHOR

Two first-time TT visitors from Spain sheltered from the rain in The George on Castletown Square. Santiago Navarro (38) from San Sebastian was on a BMW GS1200 and Eduardo Cabrera (34) from Madrid on a Ducati Multistrada. "We could only make it for four days, but we like the TT, especially the respect that exists between riders of different types of bike. The Isle of Man is surprising: it's so varied with so much of interest," Eduardo said. AUTHOR

HondaDay

Sky high. The amazing Honda-sponsored Bolddog riders Samson and Dan from Norfolk in their element at Peel. DOUBLE RED

An estimated 27,000 people defied the weather to descend on Peel for Honda day, now a traditional Mad Sunday fixture in Peel. All roads into the Island's only cathedral city were jammed with traffic and motorcycles parked in every available spot.

Honda's top TT riders were on hand to meet fans and sign autographs, while the company's amazing walking and talking humanoid robot Asimo made personal appearances. The exceptional two-man Bolddogs Lings Freestyle Team performed motorcycle aerobatics, the Animal Braun Cruzer3 Bike Tour worked miracles on Mountain bikes and the Purple Helmets presented a display of precision idiocy, their heavy macs being appropriate wear on this occasion. High speed car parking expert Russ Swift did his popular routine and live music was provided by bands, including Crash, fronted by multi-talented Manx resident James Toseland, leader of the World Superbike series on a Hannspree Ten Kate Honda.

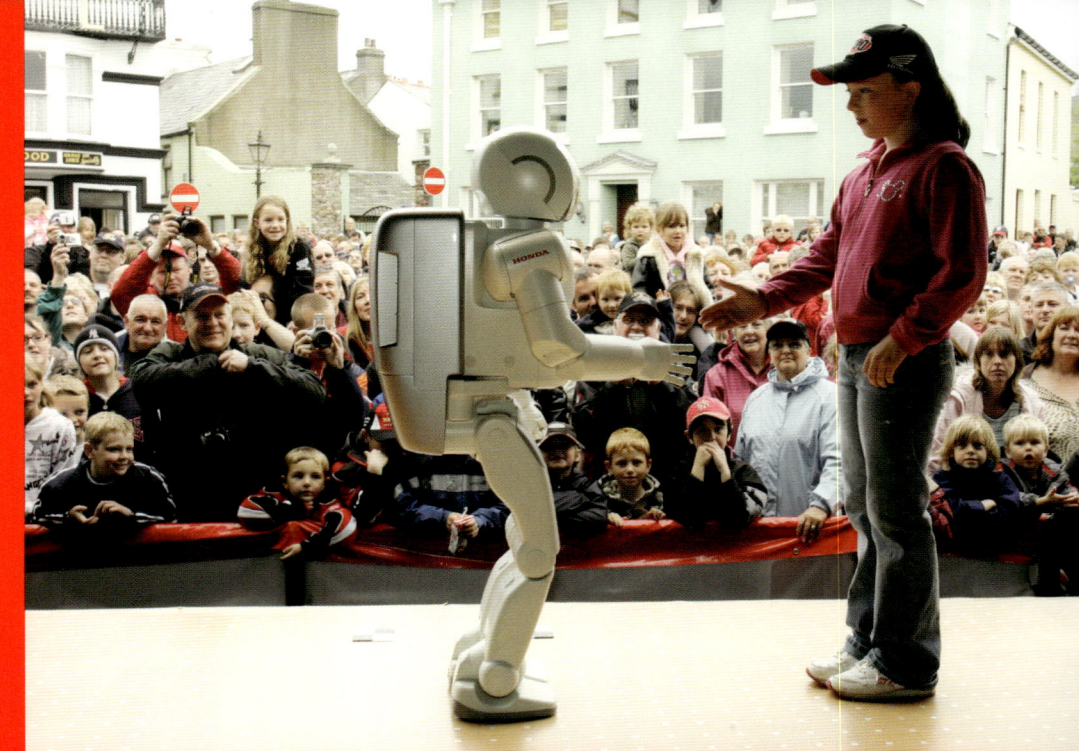

Warm technology: Honda's humanoid robot Asimo makes a new friend. DOUBLE RED

Who'd be the one in the middle? The Purple Helmets entertain. SIMON PARK

Crash's lead singer James Toseland. He's also handy on a bike. DAVE COLLISTER

Lunching in style by the yacht harbour. SIMON PARK

Peel's a Mecca for sailing and cruising, or is it baling and boozing? SIMON PARK

Suzuki Sunday

Mattie Griffin demonstrates the stunting potential of Suzuki's freshly-released Bandit GSF1250. DOUBLE RED

Seventies' factory racers in the historic display. AUTHOR

The Golf Links Hotel on the Langness peninsula was the venue for Suzuki Sunday Owners Day, where an exciting array of machinery was on show and numerous Suzuki celebrities mingled among a crowd estimated at 4,000 with sounds provided by appropriately-named rock band Suzy and the Bandits.

Biking stars at the gathering included 1993 500cc world champion Kevin Schwantz on his first visit to the Isle of Man, Mitsui Ito, the only Japanese rider to win a TT, three-times TT winner Graeme Crosby from New Zealand and British racing heroes Chris Walker and John Reynolds. TAS Suzuki's TT aces Bruce Anstey and Adrian Archibald were signing autographs and the team dished out free samples of Relentless, the energy drink sponsoring its 2007 campaign.

Two of Suzuki's GSX-R sport bikes in special limited-edition TT Centenary livery were on show as was the pre-production 1300ccB-King, fresh from its first public appearance in the hands of John Reynolds on Douglas Promenade the previous evening. Opinions varied about the bike's styling, the angular high-level exhaust outlets being the most controversial feature .

The 2007 liquid-cooled 1250cc Bandit model was demonstrated dramatically in the hotel car park by Irish stunt specialist Mattie Griffin, who performed a series of wheelies, stoppies and powerslides.

Mitsui Itoh, winner of the 1963 50cc TT at an average of 78.8mph on a Suzuki with the company's amazing twin-cylinder 50cc racer built for 1967 – sadly, his own winning machine was scrapped. "The little bikes had a cylinder capacity the size of an egg-cup and riding them fast called for a special technique. You tucked right in behind the fairing to cut wind resistance and only used the brakes when you really had to," said Itoh, who last attended the TT in the Eighties.

Rizla Suzuki British Superbike ace Chris Walker signs autographs. DOUBLE RED

Special guest Kevin Schwantz LEFT, Suzuki TT rider Adrian Archibald RIGHT with Phillip Neill of the Relentless Suzuki by TAS team. DOUBLE RED

Yamseytown

The sun actually shone for a time in Ramsey. LILY PUBLICATIONS

The town escaped the worst of the weather until rain eventually set in late in the afternoon. Mad Sunday attractions included sprint demonstrations at the northern end of the Mooragh Promenade, serving as a warm-up the serious straight-lining stuff on Yamsey day proper the following Tuesday. Arcane Manx legislation bans competitive racing on Sundays, unless an event has to be postponed or has special dispensation, like the Pre-TT races at Billown on the previous weekend.

The Army's well-drilled Royal Artillery display team, the Flying Gunners, entertained on their Yamaha WR250F Enduro machines and prizes were on offer at a slow riding competition on Yamaha's TT125, a novice-friendly trail bike.

In Ramsey Town Hall on Parliament Square four historic Yamaha racing machines were on display. They were a selection from the Yamaha Classic Racing Team, a Holland-based collection valued at £675,000 brought to the TT by Ferry Brouwer, former mechanic to Yamaha rider Phil Read and head of Arai Europe.

'That should dry the back tyre out a bit.' Limbering up for a fast standing start on the 1/8th-mile strip. LILY PUBLICATIONS

Ramsey was re-named Yamsey for the fortnight, as it was the centre for various Yamaha promoted and sponsored events.

Shetland Vikings

Five intrepid enthusiasts loaded their bikes onto the converted fishing trawler Three Sisters and left Scalloway in the Shetland Isles at 3am on Thursday of practice week. They sailed into a force eight gale bound for the Isle of Man and the TT Centenary festival.

Their first stop was Stromness in the Orkney Islands to pick up four more passengers before rounding Cape Wrath in heavy weather to call at Ullapool to pick up two more bikers and their bikes and collect 'liquid stores'.

Beer break for Vikings. STAN BASNETT

The three and a half day voyage ended at Peel on Mad Sunday, after sailing some 700 nautical miles. The first job was to unload the six bikes and wash salt spray off them.

The Three Sisters left Peel for the return journey in beautiful weather on the evening of Senior race day. The expedition had been organised by Shetlander Leslie Johnson who, along with his crew, wore Viking helmets that emphasised the strong historic links between the islands.

Unloading at Peel. JACKIE HORNE

HilariousHelmets

Conditions were moist for the Purple Helmets' main show of the TT at the Onchan Stadium, but the stoical band of nutters did their stuff regardless and had everyone in stitches as usual. The comedy display team was formed in 1995 as a filler act to give trials artist Steve Colley breaks during his physically punishing routine. They still accompany the Colley Show, but have become world famous in their own right.

Accompanied by the bone-dry wit of commentator Derry Kissack, this year's show featured a hilarious cavalcade of TT history with a wobbling, misfiring 1907 pioneer, a Twenties' flat tanker (towing a flattened oil drum) and a literal interpretation of the Fifties' dustbin fairing. There was gory horror, too, when sadistic magician Ali Bongo amputated riders' legs with a chain-saw.

Funny they may be, but the anonymous stunt riders are seriously skilled, as was shown by a backwards aerial loop-the-loop executed on an old Honda scooterette despite the wet conditions.

Beat that, professional stunters! A back-flip, in the rain, wearing a mac, on an old Honda step-thru. DAVE COLLISTER

Conditions were tricky for the Mad Sunday trial organised by the Manx Trials Club, but the heavy rain held off until late afternoon and only affected the later starters. The event's scenic venue was at Howstrake, overlooking the sea beside the coast road from Douglas to Groudle Glen, where the international Trial des Nations has been held in the past. The field was in several classes including expert, schoolboy/girl and Pre-65 for classic machines. The best performance with 22 marks lost was by Barry Kinley from nearby Onchan, also a leading Manx Enduro competitor, riding a 300cc Gas Gas.

Buona sera

It was Italian night at the Crosby Hotel, where the MV Agusta and Benelli/Motobi Owners Clubs braved the rain. Here a 1967 600cc MV Agusta roadster comes under intense scrutiny. **TRACEY HARDING**

Greeting the fairies is said to bring luck. **DOUBLE RED**

Rocketeer: the Nosha space probe built from tar barrels and buckets. **DAVE COLLISTER**

Pizza upstairs, chips downstairs. They all enjoyed the Promenade shenigans. SIMON PARK

Steve Morton's four open megaphones deafened a few people in Douglas on Sunday afternoon. The Sheffield ex-racer ran his 1973 860cc Magni MV worth £25,000 unsilenced while on the island. "I must admit it doesn't improve the performance but it sounds great!" he said. AUTHOR

Suggs and Lee Thompson of Madness. ANDREW BARTON

Stranglers guitarist Baz Warne. ANDREW BARTON

It was a wild night at the Marquee, where two huge bands from the late Seventies and early Eighties headlined. They were whimsical north London geezers Madness and revered punk band The Stranglers, whose original member Jean-Jacques Burnel is a keen motorcyclist. The support acts were Swound, a group formed by three brothers from the Isle of Man, and Brazen.

McGuinness in

Monday 4 June

Bennetts Superbike TT

John McGuinness confirmed his right to the King of the Mountain title with a start-to-finish victory in the TT Superbike race on his 1000cc HM Plant Honda. The 35 year old Morecambe rider, who first visited the TT as a boy and grew up as a devoted admirer of the original King, 26-times winner Joey Dunlop, was clearly moved at notching up his 12th win in the first race of Centenary year.

"I've never seen so many people watching along the Course. I felt part of something special," John said after the six-lap race that he won by a substantial margin of nearly 26 seconds. His win didn't come easily, though, as the opposition were doggedly snapping at his heels and he started the race under heavy pressure to justify his crown.

Anstey's Relentless Suzuki by TAS blasts off the line, but it stopped with an electronics failure after a few miles. AUTHOR

command

John McGuinness admitted that his riding was a bit ragged to start with, but he soon settled to the tidy, controlled style he is famous for. DOUBLE RED

"It wasn't all plain sailing," John said after the garlanding ceremony. "A slide at the 13th (milestone) nearly made me jump out of my skin, and then my feet came off the pegs at Rhencullen. But I had a couple of really good runs over the Mountain."

"What really helped was having the same bike and the same crew as last year. The pits stops were brilliant and played a part in the win. After my second stop I knew I had a decent lead, so I steadied up and backed off the revs."

The vaunted 130mph barrier was not broken, but McGuinness' best lap at 128.01mph was a new TT Superbike record.

"I think I've got Brandish Corner sussed now. It's tight at first then eases out, with a weird camber. If the weather stays as fine as it is, I think we'll see the 130 later in the week for sure."

Slick pit work by the HM Plant team was a factor in John McGuinness' success. Ian Whitlow fits a new visor while Mark Beeton fills the tank and Julian Boland changes the rear wheel. It takes them about 40 seconds. AUTHOR

Guy Martin dearly wanted to win, but had to settle for a creditable second place. There were plenty of dead flies on his Hydrex Honda at the finish. DOUBLE RED

The man who pressed the King hardest was ebullient 25 year old Guy Martin (Hydrex Honda), who had been less than five seconds down on him at the end of lap one and had clawed back some time in the final stages.

"I had hoped to win, but you've got to give it to John – he's the man. We'll have to make our bike better for the Senior," said Guy, who turned into the pit lane late on his first fuel and tyre stop, almost getting tangled up with HM Plant rider Ian Hutchinson.

'Hutchy' starting Number 6 finished third, 40 seconds behind Martin (Number 8) who had dived underneath him at Ramsey Hairpin during lap three to lead him on the road.

"I was a bit cautious of damp patches on the first lap and I wish now I'd gone harder right from the off," the quietly-spoken West Yorkshire rider said.

Honda Fireblades, which respond well to modifications allowed by Superbike rules, filled the next three places, ridden by Martin Finnegan, Ian Lougher and Ryan Farquhar. The

Third placeman Ian Hutchinson howls through Glen Vine on his HM Plant Fireblade. TRACEY HARDING

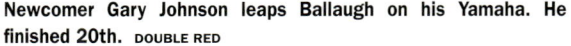

Standing tall at six foot four Conor Cummins was pround of an eighth place, averaging close to 121mph on his JMF Millsport Yamaha. AUTHOR

Newcomer Gary Johnson leaps Ballaugh on his Yamaha. He finished 20th. DOUBLE RED

machine's designer Tadao Baba, who watched the race on a flying visit to the TT, must have been pleased at the result.

The best Suzuki GSX-R1000 finisher was Adrian Archibald of the Relentless by TAS equipe, who was seventh. His team-mate Bruce Anstey had caused widespread disappointment when he dropped out of the race after only a few miles, let down by a failed electronic component.

Manxman Conor Cummins was on the first Yamaha R1 home in eight place, a fine result in distinguished company. First-timer Steve Plater could also be proud of his 10th place and his first TT silver replica, gained after he put in a fantastic 123mph final lap.

"I didn't feel under any pressure, which made it easier. I'm happy with my progress and I'm still learning. I tried new lines at a couple of places and they were wrong!" Steve said in the finishers' enclosure.

Old hands in close company. Ian Lougher (Stobart Honda 7) leads Adrian Archibald (TAS Suzuki 2), who started 50 seconds before him. They finished fifth and seventh respectively. DOUBLE RED

Manx Radio's studio in the Grandstand control tower. Anchor man Charlie Lambert and German language announcer Heike Perry LEFT hold microphones. LILY PUBLICATIONS

Hutchinson tucks himself behind the fairing as he accelerates along Glencrutchery Road at 170mph. DOUBLE RED

Winner McGuinness takes the chequered flag after averaging 125.5mph for one hour and 48 minutes. The start had been delayed while the organisers waited for hill mist to disperse. DOUBLE RED

Michael Rutter's race ended at Glen Helen on lap one and local hope Nigel Beattie was pulled off the start line three seconds before his starting time by an observant official who spotted a broken rear wheel spindle locator.

"He could have saved my life. I'm glad I didn't go off down Bray Hill with it like that," Beattie said.

Paul Hunt crashed heavily on the first lap at Kerrowmooar, recording the incident with the TV camera fixed on his Yamaha. He was airlifted to hospital but discharged next day. Mark Parrett came to grief at Cruickshanks Corner, Ramsey when in tenth place, luckily without injury. John Crellin dropped his Suzuki at the Gooseneck, was allowed to proceed, then black-flagged to leave the Course at the Grandstand.

John McGuinness was too level-headed a rider to push for the glory of a 130mph lap when he didn't need it to win the race. But even without that barrier being broken, the sunny TT Superbike was a great opening event and the fact that 120mph laps were needed to finish in the first 20 showed the tremendous standard of riding.

Bennetts *Superbike TT*

1	John McGuinness	H M Plant Honda	1h 48m 11.17s	125.550mph
2	Guy Martin	Hydrex Honda	1h 48m 37.11s	125.051mph
3	Ian Hutchinson	H M Plant Honda	1h 49m 17.33s	124.284mph
4	Martin Finnegan	Alpha Boilers Racing Honda	1h 49m 35.71s	123.936mph
5	Ian Lougher	Stobart Honda	1h 50m 34.23s	122.843mph
6	Ryan Farquhar	Mark Johns Honda	1h 50m 54.77s	122.464mph
7	Adrian Archibald	TAS Suzuki	1h 51m 27.25s	121.869mph
8	Conor Cummins	Millsport Yamaha	1h 52m 19.00s	120.933mph
9	Ian Armstrong	Canteen Smithy Yamaha	1h 53m 07.65s	120.066mph
10	Steve Plater	AIM Yamaha	1h 53m 30.84s	119.657mph

ALL THE ABOVE RECEIVED SILVER REPLICAS

11	John Barton	Marks Bloom Honda	1h 53m 49.94s	119.323mph
12	Dan Stewart	Wilcock Consulting Yamaha	1h 54m 06.19s	119.040mph
13	Chris Palmer	Solway Slate & Tile Yamaha	1h 54m 13.34s	118.915mph
14	Keith Amor	Duncan/Robinson Concrete Honda	1h 54m 21.21s	118.779mph
15	Davy Morgan	Investasure Honda	1h 54m 23.65s	118.737mph
16	Gary Carswell	Bolliger Kawasaki	1h 54m 33.53s	118.566mph
17	Ian Pattinson	Martin Bullock Raceteam Suzuki	1h 54m 34.06s	118.557mph
18	James McBride	Yamaha	1h 54m 34.61s	118.548mph
19	Stephen Oates	Hallett Aviation Suzuki	1h 55m 12.92s	117.891mph
20	Gary Johnson	Speedfreak Racing Yamaha	1h 55m 43.39s	117.373mph
21	Phil Stewart	Yamaha	1h 55m 47.05s	117.311mph
22	Les Shand	Barron Transport Honda	1h 56m 34.80s	116.511mph
23	Paul Dobbs	Dave East Suzuki	1h 56m 44.25s	116.353mph
24	Craig Atkinson	Martin Bullock Raceteam Suzuki	1h 56m 49.69s	116.263mph
25	Michael Dunlop	Yamaha	1h 57m 14.17s	115.859mph
26	Mark Miller	Wolfman/Padgetts Aprilia	1h 57m 15.61s	115.835mph
27	George Spence	Yamaha	1h 57m 46.92s	115.321mph
28	Tim Maher	Suzuki	1h 57m 59.20s	115.121mph
29	David Coughlan	Marks Bloom Yamaha	1h 57m 59.51s	115.116mph
30	Stephen Harper	Suzuki	1h 58m 14.66s	114.871mph
31	Dave Madsen-Mygdal	CSC Racing Yamaha	1h 58m 20.52s	114.776mph
32	Frank Spenner	ADAC Hessen-Thueringen Yamaha	1h 58m 34.97s	114.543mph
33	Jimmy Moore	Black Horse Honda	1h 58m 39.11s	114.476mph
34	Steve Kuenne	Sandlan Yamaha	1h 58m 54.00s	114.237mph

ALL THE ABOVE RECEIVED BRONZE REPLICAS

35	David Paredes	Bill Smith Yamaha	1h 59m 06.06s	114.044mph
36	Paul Shoesmith	Speedfreak Racing Yamaha	1h 59m 09.53s	113.989mph
37	Roger Maher	Yamaha	1h 59m 16.01s	113.886mph
38	Paul Duckett	Wilson & Collins Kawasaki	1h 59m 26.55s	113.718mph
39	Chris McGahan	McKinstry Yamaha	1h 59m 32.05s	113.631mph
40	Fabrice Miguet	Suzuki	1h 59m 43.09s	113.456mph
41	Martin Hamberg	Hallett Aviation Yamaha	1h 59m 57.51s	113.229mph
42	David Milling	Aprilia	2h 00m 17.77s	112.911mph
43	Christer Miinin	Martin Bullock Raceteam Suzuki	2h 00m 22.05s	112.844mph
44	Alan Connor	Dunshaughlin RRS Suzuki	2h 00m 27.36s	112.761mph
45	Alan Bud Jackson	BDS Fuels Suzuki	2h 00m 39.77s	112.568mph
46	Thomas Schonfelder	ADAC Hessen-Thueringen Suzuki	2h 00m 43.34s	112.513mph
47	Marc Ramsbotham	Suzuki	2h 00m 47.12s	112.454mph
48	Karsten Schmidt	Suzuki	2h 01m 18.49s	111.969mph
49	Andrew Marsden	Yamaha	2h 01m 45.13s	111.561mph
50	Sandor Bitter	Suzuki	2h 02m 35.54s	110.797mph
51	Chris Petty	York Suzuki Centre Suzuki	2h 02m 49.96s	110.580mph
52	Ian Mackman	Bill Smith Suzuki	2h 03m 03.75s	110.373mph
53	David Hewson	Kawasaki	2h 03m 12.43s	110.244mph
54	Dirk Kaletsch	Honda	2h 03m 42.85s	109.792mph
55	Antonio Maeso	Yamaha	2h 09m 09.62s	105.162mph

FASTEST LAP: JOHN McGUINNESS – 17M 38.85S; 128.279MPH ON LAP THREE (NEW RECORD)

Molyneux wins against the odds

Bavaria Sidecar TT, Race A

Molyneux and Sayle on their 'slow' Honda outfit by
the River Neb at Black Dub. DAVE COLLISTER

Andy Laidlow and Patrick Farrance slither round Quarterbridge ahead of Gary Horspole and Mark Cox. The paint on Laidlow's Suzuki LCR is a tribute to Scottish sidecar legend Jock Taylor who won four TTs between 1980 and 1982. DOUBLE RED

Dave Molyneux is rarely speechless, but he was temporarily nonplussed by a victory in the first Sidecar race that took his total of TT wins to 12. After a winter spent fighting to overcome injuries sustained in practice for the 2006 TT and a desperately unhappy practice period this year, Moly's prospects for victory had been bleak.

"It's dead weird," he said, when he eventually found words in the winners' enclosure. "I told people I'd be happy with sixth. I thought Nick (Crowe) had it in the bag. That's the most unexpected win I've ever had."

Crowe and his passenger Dan Sayle, the fastest team in practice by a fair margin, dropped out on the first lap with gearbox failure. Moly then secured his victory through sheer determination and Course knowledge accumulated since his first TT of 1985.

After hitting engine troubles in practice he was using a near-standard Honda CBR600 engine which, he claimed, was the least powerful he'd had in his own-built DMR chassis for 10 years. Nevertheless, he held second place for two of the three laps and a titanic effort to maintain his speed in corners saw Moly go from trailing John Holden's Suzuki outfit by 26 seconds at Ramsey on the first lap to a lead of 6.5 seconds at the chequered flag.

That was good! Best newcomer team driver Dougie Wright LEFT and passenger Dipesh Chauhan. AUTHOR

Crowe covered only half of the first lap before pulling in at the Sulby Glen pub, where Sayle's mother is the landlady. That handed the lead over Molyneux to Holden, while Steve Norbury disputed third spot with fellow Yamaha driver Simon Neary. Another of the fast outfits, Klaus Klaffenbock's Alpha Boilers-sponsored Honda LCR, expired at Ballacraine after only seven miles.

At the post-race press conference Molyneux said: "I rode my heart out, going round bends faster than ever before." He expressed sympathy for his protégée Nick Crowe and his gratitude to his principal sponsor Peter Lloyd, owner of the Lloyds Pharmacy chain.

Seasoned passenger Rick Long, a Peterborough-based operating theatre technician in his first season as Moly's ballast, said he was delighted to clinch his seventh TT win as a passenger. His previous successes were with Rob Fisher between 1997 and 2000.

John Holden, from Clitheroe, Lancashire and his passenger Andrew Winkle, a postman from Stoke, were pleased to be on the podium again after being third in this race in 2006.

"I saw a board saying +12, rolled it off a bit, and the next thing we were being shown –2," John said.

Steve Norbury, completing his tenth TT explained that he'd left his engine in basic tune for reliability. His passenger Scott Parnell said how glad he was to be racing in 2007:

"Last year I was lying in a Croatian hospital after hitting an Armco barrier at Rjyeka. I thought my career was finished at the time and I have to thank Dave Molyneux for putting me in touch with medical help."

Fourth placed Simon Neary from Leeds complained that the engine in his Tony Baker chassis was flat, while veteran Roy Hanks, a rostrum finisher last year, quipped "my old BSA was quicker!" when he came in twelfth on his Suzuki-powered DMR.

One of the finest performances in the race was the 17th place secured by newcomers Dougie Wright and Dipash Chauhan. The son of veteran charioteer Eddy Wright, 23 year old Dougie runs a Triumph dealership in Leeds where passenger 'Dips', a friend since school days, works as parts and accessories manager. He reported having to loosen the petrol cap occasionally to relieve pressure build-up in the tank.

The engines in the first three outfits were of three different makes, the first time this has happened in a Sidecar TT since 1992.

Molyneux hugs passenger Rick Long in the finishers enclosure.
DOUBLE RED

A stunned Dave Molyneux still can't believe he's won as his passenger Rick Long chats with Andrew Winkle, ballast for second placed driver John Holden on the rostrum. DOUBLE RED

Bavaria Sidecar TT Race A

1	Dave Molyneux/Rick Long	H M Plant Honda	1h 00m 49.06s	111.668mph
2	John Holden/Andrew Winkle	Suzuki	1h 00m 55.56s	111.470mph
3	Steve Norbury/Scott Parnell	Lockside Yamaha	1h 01m 19.73s	110.737mph
4	Simon Neary/Stuart Bond	Neary Yamaha	1h 01m 43.11s	110.038mph
5	Allan Schofield/Peter Founds	Suzuki	1m 01h 44.97s	109.983mph
6	Nigel Connole/Jamie Winn	Honda	1h 02m 20.23s	108.946mph
7	Conrad Harrison/Kerry Williams	Printing Roller Honda	1h 02m 32.54s	108.589mph
8	Tony Elmer/Darren Marshall	Elmer Yamaha	1h 02m 49.49s	108.101mph
9	Glyn Jones/Chris Lake	DSC Racing Honda	1h 03m 18.12s	107.286mph
10	Andy Laidlow/Patrick Farrance	Suzuki	1h 03m 20.19s	107.227mph
11	Gary Bryan/Ivan Murray	Yamaha	1h 03m 30.66s	106.933mph
12	Roy Hanks/Dave Wells	Suzuki	1h 03m 48.57s	106.432mph

ALL THE ABOVE RECEIVED SILVER REPLICAS

13	Brian Kelly/Dicky Gale	Honda	1h 04m 35.14s	105.153mph
14	Kenny Howles/Doug Jewell	Price Racing Suzuki	1h 04m 38.62s	105.059mph
15	Nev Jones/Joe Shardlow	Suzuki	1h 04m 44.74s	104.893mph
16	Mark Halliday/Mark Holland	Hazels Fashions Kawasaki	1h 04m 52.28s	104.690mph
17	Douglas Wright/Dipash Chauhan	Wright Honda	1h 04m 53.23s	104.665mph
18	Roger Stockton/Pete Alton	Yamaha	1h 05m 06.60s	104.307mph
19	Neil Kelly/Jason O'Connor	Honda	1h 05m 16.00s	104.056mph
20	Howard Baker/Nigel Barlow	D & J Bikespares Honda	1h 05m 35.77s	103.534mph
21	Tony Thirkell/Roy King	Merlin Race Paint Honda	1h 05m 50.50s	103.148mph
22	Bill Currie/Philip Bridge	Yamaha	1h 06m 00.87s	102.878mph
23	Mike Cookson/Kris Hibberd	Honda	1h 06m 06.32s	102.736mph

ALL THE ABOVE RECEIVED BRONZE REPLICAS

24	Peter Farrelly/Jason Miller	Yamaha	1h 07m 06.60s	101.198mph
25	Steven Coombes/Darren Hope	Ireson Honda	1h 07m 28.17s	100.659mph
26	Alan Langton/Christian Chaigneau	Sansbury Yamaha	1h 07m 30.82s	100.593mph
27	Eddy Wright/Martin Hull	Honda	1h 07m 35.17s	100.485mph
28	Peter Allebone/Bob Dowty	Kawasaki	1h 07m 35.19s	100.485mph
29	Bryan Pedder/Rod Steadman	C & C Yamaha	1h 08m 20.98s	99.363mph
30	Geoff Smale/Karl McGrath	Ireson Honda	1h 08m 33.87s	99.051mph
31	Keith Walters/James Hibberd	Honda	1h 08m 37.68s	98.960mph
32	Claude Montagnier/Laurent Seyeux	Kawasaki	1h 09m 11.07s	98.164mph
33	Michael Thompson/Bruce Moore	Yamaha	1h 09m 16.70s	98.031mph
34	Dick Tapken/Willem Vandis	Dialled In Racing Suzuki	1h 09m 32.93s	97.649mph
35	Wayne Lockey/Stuart Stobbart	Yamaha	1h 09m 45.96s	97.345mph
36	Eckhard Rossinger/Peter Hoss	Suzuki	1h 09m 59.66s	97.028mph
37	Robert Handcock/Mathew Buckley	Yamaha	1h 10m 19.14s	96.580mph
38	Brian Alflatt/Herve Chenu	Honda	1h 10m 28.40s	96.368mph
39	Masahito Watanabe/Hideyuki Yoshida	Rising Sun Racing Honda	1h 12m 28.34s	93.710mph
40	Peter Nuttall/Neil Wheatley	Honda	1h 12m 43.64s	93.382mph
41	Colin Smith/Tony Palacio	Honda	1h 14m 00.21s	91.771mph
42	Dick Hawes/Tim Dixon	Dialled In Racing Suzuki	1h 14m 35.76s	91.042mph
43	Jean-Louis Hergott/Christophe Darras	Suzuki	1h 18m 55.98s	86.040mph

FASTEST LAP: DAVE MOLYNEUX/RICK LONG – 20M 04.83S; 112.736 MPH ON LAP ONE

Afternoon Tea

Great spectating at Braddan Bridge. **LILY PUBLICATIONS**

The left-right-left set of bends at Braddan Bridge, two miles from the start, offer great views of the racing and are accessible by backroads when the Course is closed. There are two separate pay-to-enter enclosures and one, in the grounds of Kirk Braddan Parish Church SEEN TO THE RIGHT has an attraction that brings people back year upon year.

Homemade soups, freshly made sandwiches, homemade cakes and other delicious confectionery are served along with hot drinks in the Church Hall with the proceeds going to the church funds.

Relief road

Traffic queues on a red light at the entry to the access road at Quarterbridge. The route used when the roads are closed follows a disused railway line and takes vehicles under the Course at Braddan Bridge to access places inside the circuit, including Nobles Hospital. Traffic signals are used when an ambulance needs to traverse the route. **LILY PUBLICATIONS**

Panagiotis Zarifopoulos LEFT, Yla Galana MIDDLE and Panagiotis Mariolopoulos from Greece were at the TT in their capacity as new owners of the Matchless marque, which won the original Tourist Trophy race in 1907. They revealed plans to manufacture all-new Matchless motorcycles, the first of the brand to be made for 20 years. AUTHOR

PORT ERIN FUN DAY

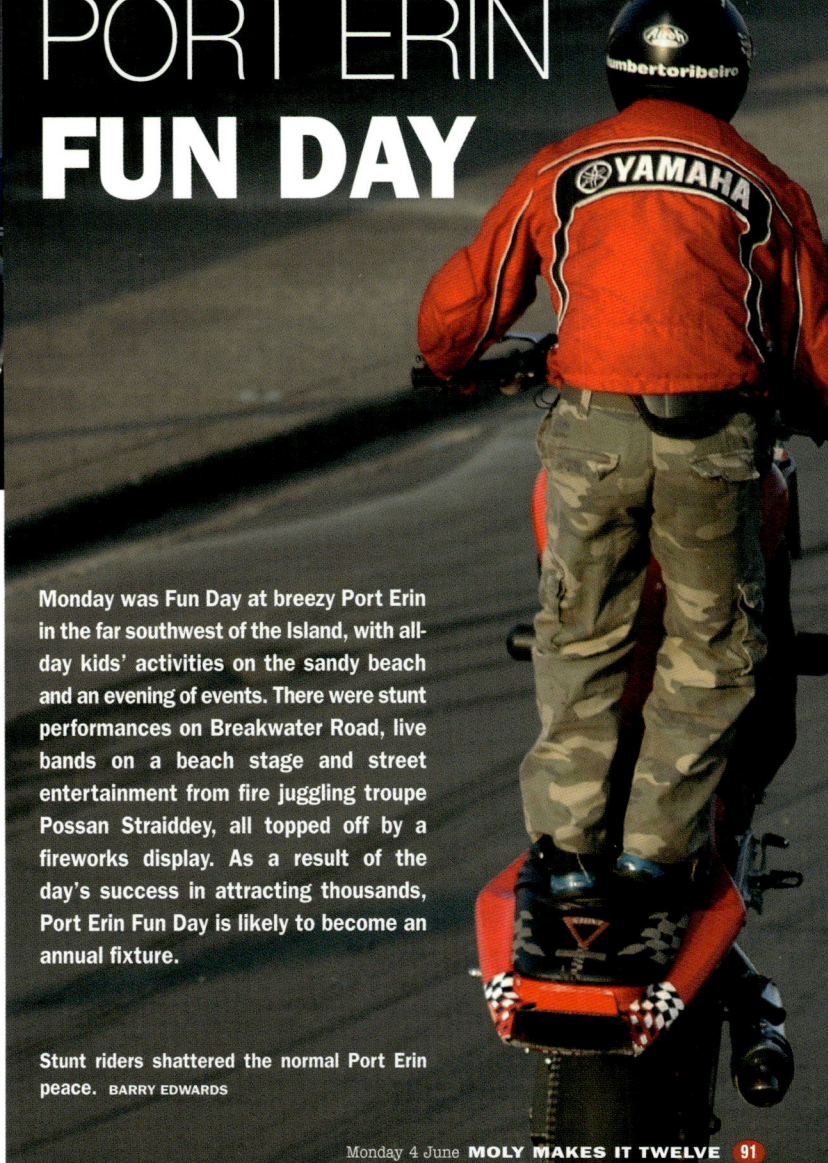

Monday was Fun Day at breezy Port Erin in the far southwest of the Island, with all-day kids' activities on the sandy beach and an evening of events. There were stunt performances on Breakwater Road, live bands on a beach stage and street entertainment from fire juggling troupe Possan Straiddey, all topped off by a fireworks display. As a result of the day's success in attracting thousands, Port Erin Fun Day is likely to become an annual fixture.

Stunt riders shattered the normal Port Erin peace. **BARRY EDWARDS**

Bushy's Brewery sold 150,000 pints over the fortnight. SIMON PARK

The Second Coming? No, just those Purple Helmets again. SIMON PARK

Edgy: Ashley Mark, a new stunt act at the TT, wears armour under his casuals. He performed nightly outside Bushy's tent. SIMON PARK

Peel Bay *Festival*

Mop-top soundalikes. ANDREW BARTON

Monday was tribute bands night, with the Bootleg Beatles and the Counterfeit Stones. Local bands 9 Bar Gypsies and Hit the North played in support.

Rolling clones. ANDREW BARTON

OLD ROAD

MOUNTAIN COURSE
5
MILESTONE
Arai

Tuesday 5 June

Anstey on the attack

PokerStars
Superstock TT

'Mr Superstock' Bruce Anstey swings his Suzuki GSX-R1000 round Creg-ny-Baa on his way to a record-breaking victory. DOUBLE RED

Quiet New Zealander Bruce Anstey came over loud and clear with a convincing win in the four-lap Superstock race.

He grabbed an early lead, gunning the big Relentless-sponsored TAS Suzuki GSX-R1000 round on a sizzling 128.297 opening lap, annihilating the class record. Stoking up the pace even more on lap two he flashed through the Sulby speed trap at 182.9mph, took the lead on the road from Honda Fireblade rider John McGuinness and led him by more than 23 seconds as the leaders pulled in for their half-distance refuelling stops. The leader's second circuit not only raised the Superstock record to an awesome 128.4mph, it also bettered the Superbike record set the day before.

Two highly placed riders failed to reach their pits. Guy Martin (Hydrex Honda Fireblade) ran out of fuel coming down the Mountain soon after being confirmed as in third position and Ryan Farquhar ran dry at Bedstead Corner when holding fifth. Superstock tanks are often 'blown' with compressed air to maximise capacity, but, in the anger of racing, riders can get drastically reduced mpg compared with practice.

Martin Finnegan proved the MV Agusta's competitiveness in Superstock by holding fourth place, pitting at the same time as third placeman Ian Hutchinson on his HM Plant Honda Fireblade.

John McGuinness (Honda Fireblade) rode hard in pursuit of Anstey to take second place. DOUBLE RED

Martin Finnegan gave MV Agusta its best TT result for 35 years, finishing fourth on the F4 1000. LILY PUBLICATIONS

On the tree-lined approach to Ramsey where Anstey (5) overtook John McGuinness (3), who started 20 seconds before him, on the second lap. DAVE COLLISTER

Gary Johnson was best newcomer, finishing 12th on a Yamaha sponsored by Cheshire's Speedfreak Racing and averaging more than 120mph. "I took it steady on the first lap, then decided to go for it," he said, admitting that he had been up eating curry and chips after midnight. The 26 year old electrician from Broughton, Lincolnshire, who went to school with Guy Martin hopes to ride for a bigger team in future. AUTHOR

Behind them there was some furious jostling for positions. Mark Parrett, apparently none the worse for his previous day's spill, was contending with fellow Yamaha R1 rider Conor Cummins who made the fastest ever lap by a Manx rider at 124.21mph on his second circuit. James McBride, Dan Stewart, Ian Armstrong and Ian Pattinson were all pressing on hard, too.

"He's Mr Superstock," Philip Neill of the Relentless Suzuki by TAS team said proudly of their winner. It was true: Anstey has won all three Superstock races run at the TT since 2005.

"The handling might have been better, but the bike went really well and I went hard for the first two laps. I seem to get on with road bikes," Bruce said in the press conference, adding that it was good to win when there were so many other antipodeans on the Island. Some racers are wary of the street bikes' stock tyres and suspension, but the big Suzuki is known to be fast and strong in relatively standard trim.

"Bruce pulled our pants down on the first couple of laps," admitted John McGuinness, who nevertheless proved the Fireblade's Superstock capability by finishing second, as did 'Hutchy' with his third on a similar Honda.

Glen Auldyn

DO NOT CROSS THE ROAD WHILST RACING IS IN PROGRESS

RIGHT
Former motocrosser Dan Stewart brought his Yamaha R1 home in twelfth place.
DOUBLE RED

LEFT
Watching from a homemade hospitality suite. STAN BASNETT

Ian Hutchinson (Honda Fireblade) drives out of Ballaugh village ahead of Martin Finnegan.... STAN BASNETT

...and they're still together at Milntown. Hutchinson finished third, while Finnegan said he'd lost time with two scary front wheel slides. DAVE COLLISTER

Aprilia dealer Dave Milling on one of the thundering Italian twins. His clutch failed on lap three. DOUBLE RED

McGuinness stands up 190kg of 1000cc Honda on the rise after Bray Hill. DOUBLE RED

Finnegan cursed a suspected deflated tyre as he got off his MV, but he had secured fourth with the fastest-ever TT race for the marque, at an average of 123.519mph. Cummins, who headed Parrett to take fifth place, said: "I'm chuffed with that result. The bike (a Millsport Yamaha R1) was tip-top." However, his reign as fastest Manxman had been short-lived as Gary Carswell, who like Cummins lives in the Ramsey area, turned in a scintillating last lap at 124.621mph to take the honour.

During the race two-times TT winner Shaun Harris (43) crashed heavily on his Blacks Suzuki at Union Mills and suffered leg and pelvic injuries. In a critical condition at first, he was making a recovery at the time of writing.

Conor Cummins (Yamaha R1) leads Ian Pattinson (Suzuki GSX-R1000) at Creg-ny-Baa. Cummins finished fifth, Pattinson eighth. DOUBLE RED

Barton bows out

"When I finished that race I had decided not to ride the 1000s and 600s in the TT any more. I wasn't enjoying it as much as in the past. But if they brought in some classes for smaller bikes, I'd definitely have a go," said John Barton, who lapped at over 122mph to take 11th place in the Superbike and was 36th in the Superstock on his 38th birthday. He withdrew from the Supersport Junior and Senior races.

A man in control: start-to-finish winner Bruce Anstey heels round the Governor's Bridge hairpin. DOUBLE RED

CONGRATULATIONS!

The media pack focus on Anstey and the Relentless Suzuki team. DOUBLE RED

PokerStars *Superstock TT*

1	Bruce Anstey	TAS Suzuki	1h 11m 56.29s	125.875mph
2	John McGuinness	H M Plant Honda	1h 12m 36.59s	124.710mph
3	Ian Hutchinson	H M Plant Honda	1h 12m 58.91s	124.075mph
4	Martin Finnegan	Alpha Boilers Racing MV Agusta	1h 13m 18.61s	123.519mph
5	Conor Cummins	Team Millsport Yamaha	1h 14m 00.26s	122.360mph
6	Mark Parrett	C & C Yamaha	1h 14m 03.65s	122.267mph
7	James McBride	Yamaha	1h 14m 21.17s	121.787mph
8	Ian Pattinson	Martin Bullock Raceteam Suzuki	1h 14m 24.54s	121.695mph
9	Gary Carswell	Suzuki	1h 14m 51.91s	120.953mph
10	Dan Stewart	Wilcock Consulting Yamaha	1h 14m 53.32s	120.915mph
11	Ian Armstrong	Powersport Suzuki	1h 15m 03.51s	120.642mph
12	Gary Johnson	Speedfreak Racing Yamaha	1h 15m 16.11s	120.305mph
13	Nigel Beattie	CD Racing/Millsport Yamaha	1h 15m 21.68s	120.157mph
14	Ian Lougher	Black Horse Honda	1h 15m 28.81s	119.968mph
15	Steve Plater	AIM Racing Yamaha	1h 15m 30.20s	119.931mph

ALL THE ABOVE RECEIVED SILVER REPLICAS

16	Stephen Oates	Hallett Aviation Suzuki	1h 15m 40.08s	119.670mph
17	Mark Buckley	Crossan Yamaha	1h 15m 40.90s	119.649mph
18	Keith Amor	Site Welding Service Honda	1h 15m 46.37s	119.505mph
19	Les Shand	Leeds Parcel Yamaha	1h 16m 06.09s	118.988mph
20	Chris Palmer	NCT Racing Yamaha	1h 16m 06.67s	118.973mph
21	Paul Dobbs	Dave East Engineers Suzuki	1h 16m 32.94s	118.293mph
22	David Coughlan	R & C Suzuki	1h 16m 45.01s	117.983mph
23	Stefano Bonetti	Suzuki	1h 17m 01.97s	117.550mph
24	Mark Miller	Wolfman/Yo Shiharu/Padgetts Aprilia	1h 17m 08.45s	117.385mph
25	Jimmy Moore	Black Horse Honda	1h 17m 09.47s	117.359mph
26	Paul Shoesmith	Speedfreak Racing Yamaha	1h 17m 10.36s	117.337mph
27	Frank Spenner	ADAC Hessen-Thuer Yamaha	1h 17m 14.25s	117.238mph
28	Paul Owen	Kawasaki	1h 17m 15.47s	117.208mph
29	Steve Kuenne	Sandlan Yamaha	1h 17m 33.17s	116.762mph
30	George Spence	Yamaha	1h 17m 39.46s	116.604mph
31	John Burrows	HM Sports Motor Suzuki	1h 17m 39.99s	116.591mph
32	Stephen Harper	Suzuki	1h 17m 53.81s	116.246mph
33	Liam Quinn	Yamaha	1h 18m 00.60s	116.077mph
34	Tim Poole	Bill Smith Yamaha	1h 18m 00.80s	116.073mph
35	Dave Madsen-Mygdal	CSC Racing Yamaha	1h 18m 06.87s	115.922mph
36	John Barton	Marks Bloom Racing Suzuki	1h 18m 33.21s	115.274mph
37	James Edmeades	Speedfreak Racing Yamaha	1h 18m 37.87s	115.161mph
38	Ian Mackman	Bill Smith Suzuki	1h 18m 38.86s	115.136mph
39	Christer Miinin	Martin Bullock Raceteam Suzuki	1h 18m 38.94s	115.134mph
40	David Paredes	Bill Smith Yamaha	1h 18m 51.83s	114.821mph

ALL THE ABOVE RECEIVED BRONZE REPLICAS

41	John Crellin	J Richards Honda	1h 19m 16.01s	114.237mph
42	Marc Ramsbotham	Suzuki	1h 19m 18.61s	114.175mph
43	Alan Connor	Dunshaughlin RRS Suzuki	1h 19m 20.83s	114.121mph
44	Alan Bud Jackson	BDS Fuels Suzuki	1h 19m 21.86s	114.097mph
45	Thomas Schoenfelder	ADAC Hessent-Thueringen Suzuki	1h 19m 30.77s	113.884mph
46	Chris McGahan	McKinstry Yamaha	1h 19m 32.22s	113.849mph
47	Robert Barber	Suzuki	1h 19m 52.03s	113.378mph
48	Fabrice Miguet	Suzuki	1h 19m 56.14s	113.281mph
49	Mike Crellin	Honda	1h 20m 49.35s	112.038mph
50	Derran Slous	Suzuki	1h 20m 49.56s	112.033mph
51	Andrew Marsden	Yamaha	1h 20m 51.94s	111.978mph
52	Chris Petty	York Suzuki Centre Suzuki	1h 21m 00.27s	111.786mph
53	David Hewson	Kawasaki	1h 21m 39.06s	110.901mph
54	Mike Hose	Aprilia	1h 22m 11.35s	110.175mph
55	Antonio Maeso	Yamaha	1h 23m 23.79s	108.580mph
56	John Nisill	PR Haulage/CJN Yamaha	1h 24m 19.37s	107.387mph
57	Bob Collins	2Bob Racing Suzuki	1h 24m 26.33s	107.240mph

FASTEST LAP: BRUCE ANSTEY – 17M 37.85S; 128.400MPH (NEW RECORD) ON LAP FIVE

Smile of a winner. DOUBLE RED

Talking to third man Hutchinson RIGHT. DOUBLE RED

Noisy lap of

After the Superstock TT race, spectators were treated to the evocative sights and sounds of the Dunlop Lap of Honour, a Mountain Course parade of former riders and guests on TT machines of the past.

Although the parade was postponed for 24 hours like the race, most of the entrants were still able to ride and around 130 took part.

Flagged away from the startline by Sixties' Sidecar TT star Colin Seeley, they included some illustrious names from TT and Grand Prix history. Luigi Taveri from Switzerland was on a rare 125cc factory Honda twin, Tommy Robb rode a replica of a 1962 works four and Jim Redman, winner of six TTs from 1963-1965 on Hondas, borrowed a modern 750cc roadster. Ex Honda and Suzuki teamster Stuart Graham had the noisiest bike of all, a faithful replica of the six-cylinder 297cc Honda used by Mike Hailwood to win the 1967 Junior.

Fuming! Roger Sutcliffe burns off excess oil in the sump of a 1939 Norton formerly displayed in The Crosby Pub. AUTHOR

Stuart Graham looks for the right gear to restart the stalled Honda Six replica. AUTHOR

John Kidson   Luigi Taveri   Jim Redman   Ernst Hiller   Dave Roper   Michelle Duff   Tommy Robb   Kel Carruthers

memories

"It was excellent," Peter Held, from Germany, who rode a fully-streamlined NSU single

Pandemonium as the loud historic machines set off in groups. Australian Barry Smith (24) is on the Production 250cc Thompson Suzuki he rode in the Sixties. He won four TTs on other machines.
LILY PUBLICATIONS

"It was like being back with and old friend," Dave Roper on the 1984 Classic TT-winning 500cc Matchless

Rob Simmons | Dieter Braun | Peter Rubatto | Stuart Graham | Tony Rutter | Ivan Rhodes | Mat Oxley | David O'Leary

"I remember these flies from years ago," Jim Redman after his lap.

"It went round as clean as a whistle," Nick Jefferies, after a lap on his 1993 Formula 1 winning 750cc Honda.

"It's still very bumpy, isn't it?" Ian Plumridge, 50cc competitor in 1963 and 1964, who paraded a 125cc Honda.

ABOVE
Dave Roper re-united with his 1984 Classic TT-winning 1959 Matchless, owned by New York's Team Obsolete. **DOUBLE RED**

ABOVE RIGHT
German collector Willi Marewski rode an ex-factory Gilera with full pre-1958 streamlining. **AUTHOR**

Those nostalgic for noisy two-stroke 'real racers' had a treat. The Yamaha Classic Racing Team fielded Canadian Michelle (formerly Mike) Duff on a 1968 250cc four, while 1969 and 1970 Lightweight winner Kel Carruthers and Rod Gould, second to Carruthers in 1970, rode factory twins.

Former MZ team rider Heinz Rosner was on a screaming 1967 twin from the old East German factory, while Tony Rutter (Michael Rutter's father and winner of seven TTs from 1973 to 1985) piloted a 350 Maxton Yamaha loaned by Phil Morris of the Road Racing Legends charity.

Mick Grant rode his Eighties' Suzuki RG500 and Bernard Murray was on a factory 500cc Yamaha raced by his one-time sponsor Barry Sheene. Both men wore their Seventies' leathers, but slim Murray's fitted him better.

There were plenty of thundering singles too. South African Paddy Driver, Tom Dickie and Keith Heckles were among those on Manx Nortons and Dave Roper, the only American to win a TT, paraded the same Team Obsolete 500cc Matchless G50 he rode to success in the one-off Classic race of 1984.

Mick Grant on his 1984 Suzuki RG500. He pulled up in Ramsey with a loose rear wheel. DOUBLE RED

Keith Heckles on the Francis Beart Norton he used to race. DOUBLE RED

Trevor Nation, who won two Production TTs and lapped at 120mph from a standing start more than 15 years ago, was on Mike Hailwood's thundering 1978 900cc Ducati Formula 1 winner, while journalist and 1985 250cc Production winner Max Oxley had a luxury ride on a 1998 Honda RC45.

The TT's traditional Lap of Honour is popular – ask officials who have to clear photographers and onlookers off the grid at the start. The Centenary event would have been better if riders were set off individually and introduced by an informative commentary. More famous riders and machines could have been assembled from Europe's thriving historic scene. Where were the rasping German BMW Rennsports that dominated the Sidecar TT from 1954 to 1974, or great Italian racing marques like Aermacchi, Benelli, Guzzi and Mondial?

One fantastic TT machine, the ex-Peter Williams Arter Matchless that was second in three Senior TTs between 1970 and 1973 stood idle because its scheduled rider had left the Island. The proposed replacement rider, winner of a 1983 Manx GP race, was not permitted to join the parade.

Trevor Nation rode Mike Hailwood's 1978 F1 winner. Mike's son David could not ride because of the one-day postponement. AUTHOR

John Davies and Ian Gemmell on the ex-Dick Hawes Seeley Matchless outfit. Its constructor Colin Seeley started the parade. DOUBLE RED

Yammy whammy

Noise to rival the bikes. The RAF's Red Arrows aerobatic display team performed over Ramsey Bay during the afternoon.
SIMON PARK

Yamsey, as Ramsey was re-named during the TT, drew big crowds for its main Yamaha-sponsored day, despite the rescheduling of the Superstock race.

The annual Ramsey Sprint meeting, held over an eighth-mile course on the North Promenade is the TT's biggest single action event outside of the Mountain Course racing.

Staged as before by sprint and drag racing promoters Straightliners, the spectacular and rowdy action attracted more than 120 riders who could enter their road bikes on the day for £35. They were literally queuing up for their turn to roar up the strip.

"Yamaha gave us 110 per cent support and we were very happy with the numbers, especially as Tuesday turned out to be a race day," Straightliners' Trevor Duckworth said.

Yamaha's special star guest for the day was two-times World Superbike champion Troy Corser from Australia, who also crammed a press conference and autograph session at the Grandstand into his flying Island visit.

One of the less frenetic Yamsey events was the Vintage Motor Cycle Club's gathering by the Mooragh Park boating lake. Best in Show was won by Richard Lancaster's rare 1924 PV Bradshaw with an oil-cooled engine, while the runner-up was a 1927 Rudge Whitworth ridden by Carol Chippendale.
SIMON PARK

Ramsey's road signs were replaced by Yamsey signs for the festival fortnight. Within days the boards, which cost £300 each, were stolen by souvenir hunters. Ramsey Town Commissioners warned that they would be watching the eBay internet auction site closely to track down the miscreants.   LILY PUBLICATIONS

Caption for top-left photo:

Straightliners
Yamsey Sprint

Top Times

Competition Unlimited		
Phil Wood	Harley Davidson	6.19secs/115mph
Richard Barks	LGF Honda	6.40secs/103mph
Stuart Harvey	Yamaha	7.32secs/97mph
Competition 750cc		
Bob Watson	Yamaha	7.30secs/96mph
Competition 500cc		
Paul Hodgson	Yamaha FZR	6.28secs/113mph
Alan Tinnion	(unspecified)	6.43secs/109mph
Steve Green	GM Special	7.02secs/98mph
SuperStreet		
Phil Wood	1300cc Suzuki Hyabusa turbo	6.11secs/122mph
Roger Simmons	1300cc Suzuki Hyabusa turbo	6.15secs/124mph
Mark Wells	1300cc Suzuki Hyabusa turbo	6.30secs/113mph
Street Legal Unlimited		
'Smokey Bacon'	1300cc Suzuki Hyabusa	6.69secs/112mph
Ben Szucs	1200cc BMW K1200R	6.79secs/111mph
'Jap'	1000cc Honda Fireblade	6.86secs/111mph
Street Legal up to 900cc		
Kevin Brock	900cc Honda Fireblade	7.21secs/103mph
Richard Penn	Kawasaki ZX6R	7.28secs/101mph
Daniel Holmes	750cc Suzuki GSX-R750	7.29secs/106mph
Street Legal up to 600cc		
Alan Tinnion	600cc Yamaha R6	6.58secs/112mph
Dave Taylor	600cc Suzuki GSX-R	7.29secs/105mph
Chris Lomo	600cc Suzuki GSX-R	7.49secs/102mph
Classic		
James Melvin	650cc Triumph	8.38secs/88mph
Julian Bunn	850cc Norton Commando	9.49secs/74mph
Richard Tracy	250cc MZ RE	10.43secs/70mph
Vintage		
John Young	500cc Triumph/JAP	8.41secs/81mph
Steve Green	500cc RVS JAP	8.73secs/78mph
Sidecar		
Father Fagan	Winstanlong Yamaha	7.84secs/80mph
Smiffy	Kawasaki ZX12R	7.92secs/97mph
James Melvin	(unspecified)	8.10secs/86mph

Human pyramid by the Yamaha-mounted Royal Artillery Flying Gunners display team. SIMON PARK

Phil Wood set the second fastest time of the day on Chester Harley-Davidson's serious 1300cc Screamin' Eagle V-Rod Destroyer. He was also fastest overall on a 1300cc turbocharged Suzuki Hyabusa, covering the eighth-mile in 6.11 seconds from a standing-start. SIMON PARK

Gems of the Yamaha Classic Racing Team at the Town Hall. Number 102 is a replica of the works 50cc RF302 built for 1969 Grands Prix but never raced. LILY PUBLICATIONS

The Grandstand beer tent is a favourite post-race rendezvous. LILY PUBLICATIONS

HONDA

EXCLUSIVE TT ISLE OF MAN

Triumphant

Cheery Harald Hahn rode to the Island from Laubach, near Frankfurt on this rusty but reliable 1953 250cc Triumph, a two-stroke single made by the German offshoot of the British Triumph company. "I'm the second owner and when I bought the bike five years ago it hadn't run for 30 years," Harald explained. AUTHOR

Discovering the back roads. BARRY EDWARDS

Riders of Oz

Western Australians at the Triumph Owners MCC gathering. Neville Crilly from Perth CENTRE WITH BEARD, owns the gigantic 2.3 litre Triumph Rocket III. He and his friends, members of R.A.T. (Riders Association of Triumph) flew their bikes to the UK for a tour including the TT. "Organising insurance was a problem until we found H & R in Aberdeen, who are fantastic," Neville said. AUTHOR

Exploring the island: a group at St John's. BARRY EDWARDS

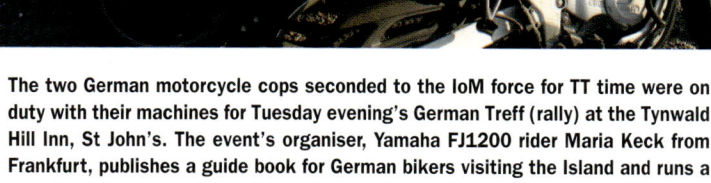

The two German motorcycle cops seconded to the IoM force for TT time were on duty with their machines for Tuesday evening's German Treff (rally) at the Tynwald Hill Inn, St John's. The event's organiser, Yamaha FJ1200 rider Maria Keck from Frankfurt, publishes a guide book for German bikers visiting the Island and runs a website at www.isle-of-man.de AUTHOR

Seaside*scramble*

Staying on is half the battle. STAN BASNETT

Results

Motorcyles Group A

1 Matthew Lund (Yamaha)
2 Gareth Quayle (Honda)
3 Will Keenan (KTM)

Group B

1 Anthony Smith (Yamaha)
2 Rob Wilson (Yamaha)
3 Gary Kirby (Yamaha)

Quads

1 Neil Kerruish (Yamaha)
2 Jamie Corkish (Honda)
3 Kevin Coole (Suzuki)

A quad capsizes. STAN BASNETT

The action was fast, furious and a touch salty at the Beach Motocross held on the shore below the Central Promenade in Douglas. Sponsored by Yamaha, the racing was organised by the Peveril MCC, which has staged TT festival support events since 1938. Taking advantage of a low tide occurring at around 9.30pm, a course was laid out with two jumps created by piling up sand with excavators. Crowds packed the promenade railings and a sizeable number risked wet feet to spectate on the shore.

Top rider of the night was reigning Manx Motocross champion Matthew Lund (Yamaha). He was fourth in his opening race after getting tangled up with a slower rider, but a win in the second leg gave him overall victory. Another local rider Anthony Smith (Yamaha) won all three Class B novice races from Scots visitor Rob Wilson.

The crowd-pleasing four-wheeler quads provided plenty of thrills and spills with Neil Kerruish (Yamaha) emerging from the sandy skirmishes as the evening's winner.

ABOVE

Only one person was permitted to park on the Prom in the evenings: precision driving wizard Russ Swift. TRACEY HARDING

On some nights 120,000 watched the entertainment. TRACEY HARDING

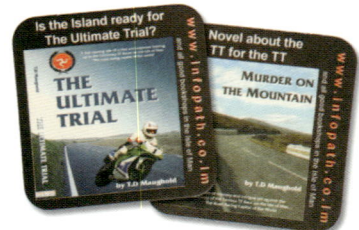

Displays by the RAF's Red Arrows aerobatic display team have been part of the TT festivities for decades. TRACEY HARDING

A change of pace. Two tall ships, the Artemis and Atlantis took passengers on sea trips. TRACEY HARDING

Peel Bay Festival

Smash hit girl group Sugababes and ex-Busted singer Matt Willis played the seventh and final night of the festival. An estimated 30,000 attended the concerts and the event's success led the organisers to suggest that it may become an annual fixture.

Walk this way! Keisha, Amelle and Heidi belt it out. ANDREW BARTON

Ian Hutchinson achieved his first TT win in the Supersport race, an exciting struggle between determined top TT riders going full-tilt on evenly-matched six-hundreds. The 27 year old 'Bingley Bullet' snatched victory on his HM Plant Honda by less than three seconds from his TT mentor John McGuinness (Padgett Honda CBR600), while Guy Martin landed third place on his Hydrex Honda after putting in the fastest lap at 125.161mph on his fourth and final circuit.

The honour of being the first rider on a 600cc machine to break the 125mph barrier went to Bruce Anstey. From the drop of the flag by guest starter Murray Walker, the Superstock TT winner screamed his TAS Suzuki GSX-R600 into the lead, completing his first lap at a record 124.055mph narrowly ahead of McGuinness, Martin and Hutchinson.

Anstey upped the pace with his sizzling 125.041mph on lap two, which included slowing for the half-distance fuel stop. But when he pressed the starter button to leave the pits, his engine refused to fire and was only coaxed into life by a long push from pit crew.

The delay proved crucial to the outcome of the closely-fought race. Anstey dropped back to fourth and Hutchinson, who had overhauled McGuinness, took over the lead while hard-charging Martin was now also ahead of the unfortunate New Zealander.

It was all action behind the leading quartet, too. Mark Parrett (Yamaha R6) had worked his way up to fifth place, pulling ahead of Ryan Farquhar (Harker Kawasaki ZX6) and Nigel Beattie (CD Yamaha R6), who were being chased furiously by Conor Cummins (Millsport Yamaha R6), Chris Palmer (Solway Honda) and best placed first-timer Steve Plater (AIM Yamaha R6) who had gained a few places by lapping at over 117mph.

Wednesday 6 June

PokerStars Supersport TT

Hutchinson proves he's a winner

"I'm ecstatic. It just shows Honda picked the right man for the job," Stuart Hutchinson, the winner's father.

Fastest man of the race Guy Martin negotiates Parliament Square's slow S-bend. DOUBLE RED

Ian Hutchinson in full flight en route to his first TT victory. DOUBLE RED

John McGuinness pushed his Padgetts Honda hard to finish second, losing one of his knee sliders in the process. DOUBLE RED

On the final run over the Mountain Hutchinson's lead from McGuinness was a mere four seconds, while Martin's record speed kept him ahead of Anstey, but only just.

McGuinness took the flag and when Hutchinson followed him in he was confirmed the winner by a slender 2.84seconds, with Martin another four seconds adrift.

It was a particularly sweet victory for Hutchinson as he had been excluded from second place in the 2006 Supersport race on a piffling camshaft technicality which he'd no knowledge of before the race.

"The race went perfectly for all four laps and when Bruce came past me at Kirk Michael I realised something must have happened to him. I went after him to re-pass: there was a lot of action going on,' Hutchy said after the finish, thanking the HM Plant Honda team for taking him on. McGuinness, who lost his HM Plant Supersport ride over the winter, thanked Padgetts for providing a competitive machine.

"I gave it everything out there," he said. "You have to keep the 600 wound right on all of the time. I clipped a knee-slider off my leathers somewhere, so I could feel my knee rubbing on the road."

Where else but the TT? A rider takes Brandish Corner, completely altered since 2006 by removing banks and easing the curve. DOUBLE RED

Consistent Conor Cummins (Yamaha) took sixth place. DOUBLE RED

Bends, bends, bends. DOUBLE RED

Newcomer Ian Mackman (Suzuki). STAN BASNETT

Martin said he'd made an effort to speed up in the latter half of the race. "I knew it was tight so I went out to do a really good last lap. I made a pig's ear of Governor's, but I hear I got the record."

Despite his superb riding Anstey had to settle for fourth and his dejection was only worsened when the Suzuki's starter was tried again in the finishers' enclosure - it fired the engine immediately.

Manx Telecom employee Nigel Beattie was more than satisfied with fifth place: "That was hard. I had a couple of slides, the worst at Laurel Bank. I saw a board held out for Conor (Cummins) so I knew that as long as I kept him in sight I'd got him. But it didn't help when the low fuel light came on at the Gooseneck on the last lap."

Irishman Ryan Farquhar, who missed the 2006 TT through injury, strove hard for success. He was seventh on a Harker Kawasaki. DOUBLE RED

Hutchinson hurtles past the Crosby pub on the long fast stretch from Glen Vine to Greeba Castle. DAVE COLLISTER

Steve Plater was justifiably pleased at another good result: eighth at an average of 120mph-plus. Another happy newcomer was Jimmy Moore, from Oregon who said it had been his best ride yet. Backed by the www.motorcycleusa-com website, the Alaska-born rider was fixed up with his Black Horse Honda ride by Ian Lougher and Paul Phillips.

Mark Parrett's race ended when he pulled in at Quarterbridge on the final lap, when lying fifth. A flattened rear tyre had given him a hair-raising ride down Bray Hill.

McGuinness LEFT **talks to unlucky Anstey.** DAVE COLLISTER

Winner 'Hutchy' flanked by John McGuinness with son Ewan LEFT Guy Martin and the PokerStars girls. DOUBLE RED

PokerStars *Supersport TT*

1	Ian Hutchinson	H M Plant Honda	1h 13m 29.11s	123.225mph
2	John McGuinness	Padgetts Honda	1h 13m 31.95s	123.145mph
3	Guy Martin	Hydrex Honda	1h 13m 35.92s	123.035mph
4	Bruce Anstey	TAS Suzuki	1h 13m 38.27s	122.969mph
5	Nigel Beattie	CD Racing/Millsport Yamaha	1h 15m 03.59s	120.640mph
6	Conor Cummins	Team Millsport Yamaha	1h 15m 10.08s	120.466mph
7	Ryan Farquhar	Harker Kawasaki	1h 15m 14.46s	120.349mph
8	Steve Plater	AIM Racing Yamaha	1h 15m 14.93s	120.337mph
9	Chris Palmer	Solway Slate & Tile Honda	1h 15m 15.20s	120.330mph
10	Ian Lougher	Black Horse Honda	1h 15m 34.94s	119.806mph
11	Dan Stewart	Wilcock Consulting Yamaha	1h 15m 41.99s	119.620mph
12	Keith Amor	Wilson Craig Honda	1h 15m 45.03s	119.540mph
13	Martin Finnegan	Alpha Boilers Racing Honda	1h 16m 05.56s	119.002mph
14	Ian Pattinson	Martin Bullock Raceteam Honda	1h 16m 08.61s	118.923mph
15	Jimmy Moore	Black Horse Honda	1h 16m 22.98s	118.550mph
16	Ian Armstrong	Padgetts Honda	1h 16m 23.94s	118.525mph
17	Roy Richardson	Ian Barnes Racing	1h 16m 34.44s	118.254mph
18	Les Shand	McKinstry Skip Hire Yamaha	1h 16m 51.20s	117.825mph
19	James McBride	Yamaha	1h 16m 51.94s	117.806mph

ALL THE ABOVE RECEIVED SILVER REPLICAS

20	Paul Dobbs	Action Triumph	1h 17m 19.07s	117.117mph
21	Gary Carswell	Crossan Motorcycles Honda	1h 17m 40.45s	116.579mph
22	Stephen Oates	Hallett Aviation Suzuki	1h 17m 40.78s	116.571mph
23	Adrian McFarland	Hardship Racing Yamaha	1h 17m 53.39s	116.256mph
24	Mark Buckley	Crossan Motorcycles Honda	1h 17m 55.99s	116.192mph
25	Tim Poole	Bill Smith Triumph	1h 18m 15.56s	115.708mph
26	Craig Atkinson	Martin Bullock Raceteam Honda	1h 18m 16.52s	115.684mph
27	Paul Owen	Rapid Racing Honda	1h 18m 32.00s	115.304mph
28	David Milling	Dave Milling Motorcycles Honda	1h 18m 34.42s	115.245mph
29	Davy Morgan	Autotech Honda	1h 18m 48.07s	114.912mph
30	Stefano Bonetti	Honda	1h 18m 53.57s	114.779mph
31	Paul Shoesmith	Speedfreak Racing Yamaha	1h 19m 18.18s	114.185mph
32	Paul Duckett	Investasure Triumph	1h 19m 32.21s	113.849mph
33	Mark Miller	Woolfman/Yo Shiharu/Padgett Honda	1h 19m 33.88s	113.809mph
34	Dave Madsen-Mygdal	CSC Racing Yamaha	1h 19m 39.73s	113.670mph
35	David Coughlan	ATM Construction Honda	1h 19m 45.08s	113.543mph
36	Chris McGahan	Manx Glass and Glazing Yamaha	1h 19m 53.68s	113.339mph
37	Alan Bennie	Honda	1h 19m 55.09s	113.306mph
38	Phil Harvey	the FSD.com Yamaha	1h 20m 02.69s	113.127mph
39	Manfred Vogl	Yamaha	1h 20m 21.78s	112.679mph
40	Karsten Schmidt	Ducati	1h 20m 22.18s	112.669mph
41	Mike Hose	Honda	1h 20m 40.98s	112.232mph
42	Thomas Schoenfelder	ADAC Hessent-Thuering Suzuki	1h 20m 46.47s	112.105mph
43	Derran Slous	Honda	1h 20m 48.81s	112.051mph

ALL THE ABOVE RECEIVED BRONZE REPLICAS

44	Stephen Harper	Honda	1h 20m 55.21s	111.903mph
45	John Crellin	Yamaha	1h 21m 09.14s	111.583mph
46	Alan Connor	Dunshaughlin Suzuki	1h 21m 18.74s	111.363mph
47	Mike Crellin	Yamaha	1h 21m 29.06s	111.128mph
48	Ian Mackman	Bill Smith Suzuki	1h 21m 33.28s	111.032mph
49	Etienne Godart	Martin Bullock Raceteam Honda	1h 21m 33.78s	111.021mph
50	Chris Petty	Dave Milling Motorcycles Honda	1h 22m 00.16s	110.426mph
51	Alan Bud Jackson	Oddfellows Racing Yamaha	1h 22m 08.31s	110.243mph
52	Phil Gilmour	Yamaha	1h 22m 30.42s	109.751mph
53	Robert Barber	Triumph	1h 22m 32.53s	109.704mph
54	Angelo Conti	Triumph	1h 22m 41.58s	109.504mph
55	Kevin Murphy	C & C Triumph	1h 24m 23.19s	107.306mph
56	John Nisill	Greenhey Racing Honda	1h 24m 51.92s	106.701mph
57	Wade Boyd	Hallett Aviation Kawasaki	1h 24m 59.66s	106.539mph

FASTEST LAP: GUY MARTIN – 18M 05.23S; 125.161MPH ON LAP FOUR

TT Tattoos proudly worn by US rider Jimmy Moore and his friend and helper Tom Kenny. They were executed by Phantom Tattoo in Centralia, Washington State – free of charge. Newcomer Moore finished 15th in the Supersport race. AUTHOR

Disaster for Crowe, *delight for Molyneux*

Bavaria
Sidecar Race B

Nick Crowe suffered his second devastating disappointment of the week in the Sidecar B race. His engine spat out a connecting rod on the third and final lap on the Ballahutchin Straight when he held a handsome lead of more than 30 seconds. The four-cylinder Honda CBR600 unit, newly assembled and run-in for the race, had been revved mercilessly by the Manx rider who did at least come away with the satisfaction of setting a new Sidecar lap record at 116.667mph.

All three wheels off the road. Molyneux and Rick Long powered to victory with a fresh engine. DOUBLE RED

The man whose record he beat, fellow local Dave Molyneux, won the race, as he had the first sidecar event on Monday. It was his thirteenth TT victory, placing him third in the all-time rankings behind Joey Dunlop with 26 wins and Mike Hailwood with 14.

For Moly's ballast Rick Long it was an eighth TT win, exceeding the old record of seven gained by German passenger Wolfgang Kalauch between 1970 and 1978. The winning team had slotted into second place during the first lap, holding off A race runner-up John Holden's Suzuki outfit and Austrian driver Klaus Klaffenbock's Honda LCR.

As the streamlined outfits screamed past the Grandstand at 140mph to end lap one, Crowe led Moly by nearly 15 seconds and he more than doubled the difference on his record – and engine-breaking second circuit. Klaffi's engine did not sound

Nick Crowe on Crosby Hill. He blew away the lap record, but his engine cried enough climbing away from Union Mills on lap three. STAN BASNETT

Dick Hawes, who first raced in the Sidecar TT in 1966 and finished third in the 1974 500cc race and third overall in the 1993 races, decided to retire from TT racing after the Sidecar B race, in which his Yamaha outfit did not finish. Originally from Essex, Dick has made the Isle of Man his home.

Gary Bryan and Ivan Murray headed for 11th place on their Yamaha outfit. DOUBLE RED

crisp and he too succumbed to mechanical trouble only a couple of miles into the last lap; a frustrating end to a difficult fortnight for a driver who has set his heart on winning a TT.

Holden, who exceeded 144mph through the Sulby speed trap, kept going strong. He could not pull any time out on the experienced Molyneux, but he kept Steve Norbury at bay. The trio finished in that order, making it a repeat of Monday's rostrum result and the next four placings were a carbon copy as well.

The start of the race had been delayed by fifteen minutes because a dog was running loose on the road near Ballagarey. When the reason was explained to Moly afterwards he said: "I don't normally like dogs, but I love that one! The extra time allowed us to change the instrument dash because the electronics were playing up. I think it was the last thing left that we hadn't changed on the bike. I never had a more difficult TT."

Moly thanked HM Plant Honda who had lent him Ian Hutchinson's spare Supersport engine for the race. He commiserated with the Crowe/Sayle team and their main sponsor Andy Faragher of AJ Groundworks.

John Holden said he'd stuck with one Suzuki engine since arriving on the Island.

"All we did to it was change the oil and filters and adjust the injection mapping. But we're well down on the power and wouldn't mind a bit of official Suzuki help," he said.

Fourth place was again taken by Allan Schofield and Dessie Founds on their Suzuki . They might have made the rostrum had they not been black flagged for a machine check at Ramsey on the last lap. Schofield, whose nickname is 'Scud', had struck Gary Horspole's outfit on Ballaugh Bridge and it overturned. After the front of his fairing was checked for damage, Schofield was able to continue but his appeal to be credited with the lost time was rejected. The far-from-happy Horsepole was taken to hospital with an arm injury but his passenger Mark Cox was unhurt.

Bavaria Sidecar TT Race B

1	Dave Molyneux/Rick Long	HM Plant Honda	59m 39.11s	113.851mph
2	John Holden/Andrew Winkle	Suzuki	1h 00m 05.26s	113.025mph
3	Steve Norbury/Scott Parnell	Lockside Yamaha	1h 01m 07.80s	111.098mph
4	Simon Neary/Stuart Bond	Neary Racing Yamaha	1h 01m 21.70s	110.678mph
5	Allan Schofield/Peter Founds	Suzuki	1h 01m 44.80s	109.988mph
6	Nigel Connole/Jamie Winn	Honda	1h 01m 49.55s	109.847mph
7	Conrad Harrison/Kerry Williams	Printing Roller Honda	1h 02m 01.81s	109.485mph
8	Glyn Jones/Chris Lake	DSC Racing Honda	1h 02m 35.84s	108.493mph
9	Tony Elmer/Darren Marshall	DL Elmer Yamaha	1h 02m 37.52s	108.445mph

ALL THE ABOVE RECEIVED SILVER REPLICAS

10	Kenny Howles/Doug Jewell	Price Racing Suzuki	1h 02m 59.14s	107.825mph
11	Gary Bryan/Ivan Murray	Baker Yamaha	1h 03m 06.02s	107.629mph
12	Andy Laidlow/Patrick Farrance	Suzuki	1h 03m 42.95s	106.589mph
13	Roger Stockton/Pete Alton	Baker Yamaha	1h 03m 47.23s	106.470mph
14	Dave Wallis/Philip Iremonger	Compass Honda	1h 04m 08.45s	105.883mph
15	Douglas Wright/Dipash Chauhan	Wright Honda	1h 04m 45.81s	104.865mph
16	Bill Currie/Philip Bridge	Yamaha	1h 04m 55.30s	104.609mph
17	Brian Kelly/Dicky Gale	DMR Honda	1h 05m 09.32s	104.234mph
18	Neil Kelly/Jason O'Connor	Honda	1h 05m 22.79s	103.876mph
19	Tony Thirkell/Roy King	Merlin Race Paint Honda	1h 05m 25.88s	103.794mph

ALL THE ABOVE RECEIVED BRONZE REPLICAS

20	Mike Cookson/Kris Hibberd	Honda	1h 05m 46.20s	103.260mph
21	Rod Bellas/Geoff Knight	Honda	1h 06m 00.99s	102.874mph
22	Eddy Wright/Martin Hull	Honda	1h 06m 02.99s	102.822mph
23	Dylan Lynch/Aaron Galligan	Honda	1h 06m 18.40s	102.424mph
24	Peter Nuttall/Neil Wheatley	Honda	1h 06m 27.14s	102.199mph
25	Francois Leblond/Sylvie Leblond	Honda	1h 06m 34.20s	102.019mph
26	Mike Roscher/Michael Hildebrand	Yamaha	1h 07m 23.73s	100.769mph
27	Eckhard Rossinger/Peter Hoss	Suzuki	1h 07m 45.14s	100.239mph
28	Bryan Pedder/Rod Steadman	C & C Yamaha	1h 07m 50.68s	100.102mph
29	Alan Langton/Christian Chaigneau	Sansbury Yamaha	1h 08m 02.72s	99.807mph
30	Claude Montagnier/Laurent Seyeux	Kawasaki	1 h08m 09.09s	99.651mph
31	Jean-Louis Hergott/Christophe Darras	Suzuki	1h 08m 15.95s	99.485mph
32	Wal Saunders/Eddy Kiff	Dialled In Racing Suzuki	1h 08m 28.42s	99.183mph
33	Wayne Lockey/Stuart Stobbart	Yamaha	1h 08m 46.35s	98.752mph
34	Alan Warner/Bert Vloemans	Dialled In Racing Kawasaki	1h 08m 53.70s	98.576mph
35	Dick Tapken/Willem Vandis	Dialled In Racing Suzuki	1h 09m 35.04s	97.600mph
36	Robert Handcock/Mathew Buckley	Baker Yamaha	1h 09m 40.12s	97.481mph
37	Geoff Smale/Karl McGrath	Self Drive Hire Honda	1h 10m 42.02s	96.059mph
38	Masahito Watanabe/Hideyuki Yoshida	Rising Sun Racing Honda	1h 11m 12.43s	95.375mph
39	Ian Salter/Deborah Salter	Honda	1h 11m 30.33s	94.977mph
40	Ruth Laidlow/Mike Killingsworth	Action Motorcycles Honda	1h 11m 44.56s	94.663mph
41	Colin Smith/Tony Palacio	Honda	1h 12m 33.98s	93.589mph
42	Peter Farrelly/Jason Miller	Yamaha	1h 12m 43.01s	93.395mph

FASTEST LAP: NICK CROWE/DAN SAYLE – 19M 24.24S; 116.667MPH ON LAP TWO

Dave Molyneux consoles friend Nick Crowe. AUTHOR

Veteran pilot Dick Hawes with Tim Dixon at Quarterbridge. DOUBLE RED

Eye in the sky

By filming from a helicopter, the Greenlight TV crew can snatch TT action that it is impossible to capture at ground level. But airborne cameraman Simon Werry, who has been filming the TT since 2004 says that shooting clear, sharp pictures of 190mph motorcycles from a 150mph helicopter can be a tough job.

The latest technology helps. Simon uses the Cineflex system with a Sony Hi-Def camera in a gimble stabliser and a lens with a super-long 840mm focal length. The whole package is valued at around £250,000.

Despite the demands, Simon enjoys working at the TT: "I relish the opportunity to be a part of this amazing race. I love the history of it all and feel privileged to have the best seat in the house," he says.

Motor sport specialist Greenlight supplied its superb aerial and ground-level footage of the 2007 TT to BBC TV, ITV4 and Duke Video.

Simon Werry at the camera controls. DAVE COLLISTER

Former German champion Heine Butz with the Italian 500cc Bianchi he raced in the Sixties. It was displayed and paraded with other fabulous historic racers taken to the TT by Team Marewski, Team Rosner and Team Schneider. AUTHOR

Daniel Jansen made a desperate appeal for financial help with repairing his Kawasaki ZX10 after a crash at Union Mills on the fifth lap of the Superbike race. The New Zealander took a pitch in the paddock marketplace with a collecting bucket in the hope of getting sorted out for Friday's Senior race, but unfortunately he wasn't able to start. AUTHOR

Francois and Sylvie Leblond were 25th in the Sidecar B race and the best of three French teams to finish. The couple from Pigeon in the Cotes du Rhone completed the race despite Francois' right-side kneeler tray breaking under the strain. AUTHOR

Japanese visitors Seiko Tamayama LEFT and Niomi Morizuka Kumicho watched the Supersport race at Braddan Bridge. "This is so different. The experience is very direct because you can get so close to the action," Seiko said. It was her first Island visit, but Niomi was at the TT 17 years ago. The pair had rented a Suzuki Bandit in London. AUTHOR

Fewtakers

The steam train and electric tram commuter services did not attract as many passengers as the Island's transport authorities had hoped. An estimated 20 customers regularly used the steam service between Port Erin and Douglas while only one non-tourist passenger was found to be taking the Manx Electric Railway, which takes more than an hour to travel from Ramsey to Douglas, on a daily basis.

Noise night
on the Prom

Crowds were treated to deafening noises from the past when the evening entertainment on Douglas Promenade was devoted to historic racing machines and some well-known TT names from the past.

Bernard Murray squirts an ex-Barry Sheene Yamaha two-stroke four along the Prom. Murray was a double Manx GP winner in 1974 and rode in the TT until 1984. SIMON PARK

Kevin Schwantz defends his ears. DAVE COLLISTER

Two of the old machines picked up speed spectacularly: Mick Grant's Kawasaki KR750 – timed at 190mph in the 1977 TT – and Heinz Rosner's sleek 1967 350cc factory MZ, both sounding fiery. Full-blooded howls came from the Kay Gilera replica demonstrated by eight-times TT winner Phil Read and some Honda Four replicas including a pair of 1967 500cc RC181 clones made in Budapest by Roland Agoston.

The Yamaha Classic Racing Team were out in force along with the German group that had participated in the Lap of Honour the day before. They ran an ex-factory NSU twin of the type that completely dominated the 1954 Lightweight TT, taking five out of the six top places. Former German champion Ernst Hiller (78) got aboard Willi Marewski's precious Gilera Four, but was caught out by the restricted steering lock when making a U-turn in front of the Sefton Hotel and it toppled over.

Star of the big screen: former MZ works rider Heinz Rosner gave his rowdy 1967 350cc twin an airing. DAVE COLLISTER

The bikes were blasted up and down the dual carriage-way in front of the Villa Marina colonnade and commentator Geoff Cannell interviewed the riders, also providing historical information about them and their machines.

A fascinating Suzuki factory racer made a sound for connoisseurs to savour when revved up by 1963 50cc TT winner Mitsui Itoh. The incredibly compact four-cylinder 125cc RT67/68 disc valve two-stroke had never previously been seen or heard outside of Japan and was only raced once, in the 1967 Japanese GP.

Ex-Suzuki teamster Stuart Graham revs a 1967 125cc four never before seen outside Japan. DAVE COLLISTER

Tony Rutter and his TT Formula 2 Ducati. Michael Rutter's father won four F2 TT races and three others. DAVE COLLISTER

Sixties' 500cc 'Honda' Fours cloned in Hungary by Roland Agoston. SIMON PARK

Two of Suzuki's star guests, 1993 500cc world champion Kevin Schwantz and three-times TT winner in 1980-1981 Graeme Crosby, shot along the Prom together, their front wheels pawing the air. Suzuki furnished them with special edition GSX-R1000s, in appropriate period paint colours; Lucky Strike style for Schwantz and Texaco Heron livery for Croz.

Later on, equally loud noises from the spectacular but rather brief fireworks display on the beach rounded off the evening.

Packed promenade. The annual French get together in mid-TT week was bigger than ever. SIMON PARK

Champions *galore*
Thursday 7 June

Ol' blue eyes is back! Former TT lap record holder Carl Fogarty is now involved with MV Agusta's World Superbike team. DAVE COLLISTER

A galaxy of motorcycle racing stars appeared at the Arai Day of Champions based at the Grandstand, where they were interviewed on the winners' rostrum by Charlie Williams and Chris Kinley of Radio TT.

Ten-times TT winner Giacomo Agostini was now on the Island, as was his MV Agusta team predecessor and six-times winner John Surtees. Famous commentator Murray Walker, whose father was a TT winner in the Thirties, had arrived in time to start Wednesday's Supersport race.

Another face known to millions at the gathering was Carl Fogarty. Winner of three TT races, 'Foggy' held the outright TT Course record at 123.61mph.from 1992 to 1999. He stopped racing at the TT after 1992 and gained massive fame by winning the World Superbike championship five times.

"I didn't want to miss this. I'm really pleased to be back," he said.

Another World Superbike star present, Noriyuki Haga from Japan, has not raced at the TT but is known to all racing fans as a fearless rider and colourful character.

Another popular personality in attendance was former TT rider and Superbikes ace Jamie Whitham. While on the Island he was doing pit work for his competitor friend Paul Shoesmith and generally helping out. British Superbike Rizla Suzuki ace Chris 'Stalker' Walker was also around the paddock.

Yanks in Manxland: Kevin Schwantz with TT first-timer Jimmy Moore, ice cream in hand. DAVE COLLISTER

Ten-times TT winner Giacomo Agostini LEFT talks to two-times winner Kel Carruthers. Both men managed teams for Yamaha after they retired from racing; Ago in Italy, Carruthers in the US. DAVE COLLISTER

1973 125cc TT winner Tommy Robb. DAVE COLLISTER

Many people must have been pleased to see Dennis Ireland back on the Isle of Man. The New Zealand rider won the 1000cc Classic race during the 75th anniversary TT in 1982 after recovering from serious injuries incurred elsewhere.

Australian Glen Richards, leader of the UK Metzeler National Superstock series, was also interviewed revealing that his father had raced in the TT on a Manx Norton.

The event raised funds for the Joey Dunlop Foundation, which exhibited some of the great man's trophies in the Mike Hailwood Centre paddock meeting room, as well as the ACU Benevolent Fund.

Sign here please! Murray Walker was in demand for autographs. DAVE COLLISTER

Manx resident Neil Hodgson signs for a fan. DAVE COLLISTER

The Road Racing Legends charity presented £3000 to the Rob Vine Fund, founded in memory of a TT rider killed in 1985 to provide medical facilities at the TT. The giant cheque was presented to Shaun Hogg MIDDLE of the Hogg Motorsport Association, set up after his brother Phil was killed practising for the 1989 TT. The Association gives medical support to all Manx automotive sport. The representatives of RRL are Phil and Gwen Morris RIGHT, while Colin Morris (no relation) holds the giant cheque and his wife Sue is on the left. AUTHOR

Laid back in Laxey

Sunny Laxey Promenade was the centre of attention on Thursday afternoon, thanks to a new TT Week event staged by the Isle of Man-based Moddey Dhoo MCC in conjunction with Laxey Village Commissioners.

CAROL BASNETT

The idea of the friendly free-to-enter Centenary TT Motorcycle Show was to invite all the various motorcycle clubs to gather in one place at the same time, as well as encouraging individual owners to put their bikes on display.

Among organisations seen at the show were the Benelli, MV Agusta, Hesketh and Honda CB1100R and CBX Owners Clubs, while a wide variety of individual machines on display ranged from ancient flat tankers to aggressive street fighters and eye-catching customs.

Local rock band Dan Gleebitz provided sounds, there was an adequate supply of hot dogs, ice cream and for anyone inclined to stroll around the corner, beer at the Shore Hotel.

Laxey Beach or Daytona Beach? MODDEY DHOO MCC

The name lives on. AUTHOR

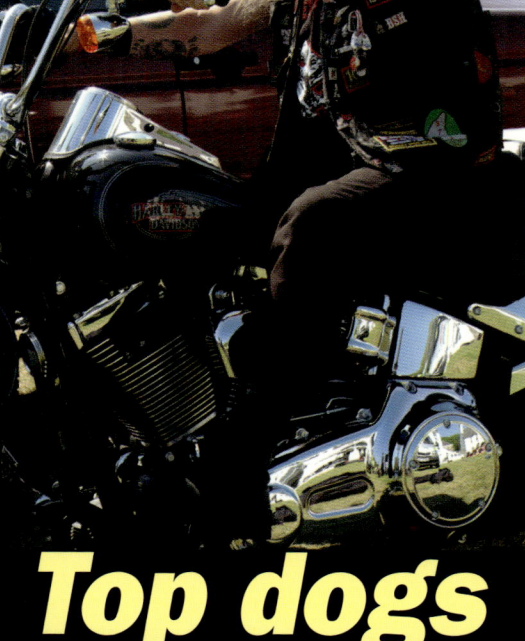

Hailwood Tribute

Top dogs

Founded in 1993 the Moddey Dhoo MCC is a custom bike and Harley-Davidson-oriented club with an emphasis on social activities. Its name, which translates from Manx Gaelic as Black Dog, comes from the legend of a malign canine ghost that haunts Peel Castle and sometimes appears elsewhere as a harbinger of doom.

Results

Superbike	Yamaha YZF R1, Paul Tupling
Touring	Honda CB 1100RC, Jan Ringnalda (USA)
Streetfighter	Suzuki GSX 1100 Turbo, John Carr
Sidecar	Kawasaki 1100, Phil, Donna & Katie-Jo
Moped	1956 Cyclemaster, Mo Simpson
Trials/Off Road	Triumph TR5T Adventurer, R Papps
Japanese	Honda CBX, John Dalton
British	1955 Triumph TR5 Trophy, Doug Webb
Italian	MV Agusta Marlboro Agostini, Ray Marchant
German	1939 BMW R61, Joe McKeown
Unspecified	Triking 3 Wheeler, Geoff Mitchell
Custom Engineering	Honda CBX, Steve Flavell
Custom Paint	Suzuki GSX (Wonder Woman), Justine Ball
Trike	'Big Black Rat Trike', Steve Beard
Race Bike	Triumph 600 Daytona No.66, Kevin 'Ago' Murphy
Drag/Sprint Bike	Yamaha FZR 1043 EXUP, Stuart Harvey
British Classic	1955 Triumph TR5 Trophy, Doug Webb
European Classic	1939 BMW R61, Joe McKeown
American Classic	Harley-Davidson 1200 Sportster, 'Jas'
Japanese Classic	Honda Six Hailwood tribute, Richard Downham
Vintage	1923 Levis, Richard Stephen
Hesketh	V1000, Dave Killner
Norton	1992 P55 F 1 Rotary race rep, (owner unknown)
Buell	1998 S1, Glyn Richards
BMW	R1150 GS (Modified)/sidecar, Lee Saunders
Harley	2003 Road King, John Cullen
Adapted for Disability	Cagiva V Raptor 1000, Shelly Hurst
Owned by a Lady Rider	Custom 'Outspan' Bike, Karen Peters
Club Stand	Ladies of Mann MCC
How the hell did it get here?	Suzuki GSX, 'Stigg'
Long Way Round Award	Paul and Gill Edlington from Auckland, New Zealand, BMW K1100 RS ridden from India
Overall Best in Show (voted by the public)	1955 Triumph TR5 Trophy, Doug Webb

Dangerous curves

The self-explanatory Curvy Riders were well represented at Laxey. The UK-wide 220-strong women bikers group was founded in 2006 and has a thriving Isle of Man section with 12 members who go on fortnightly ride-outs. AUTHOR

Sidecars *on the rocks*

Steady! Dave Haynes and Wendy Brennan (Montesa). CHRIS MOLYNEUX

Ton-up trike

Jim and Sonny Serr on their Rewaco trike at Laxey. Originally from South Dakota USA, the couple live in Oxford. They have both been lifelong bikers and when Sonny lost her sight they turned to a trike so that they can both still enjoy the sensations of riding.

"This is our first time at the TT. We came over with friends who have been coming for more than 40 years," Sonny said. The German-built Rewaco has a 1.6 litre Ford Zetec engine that can take it well over 100mph and a spacious luggage boot. Although it is not compulsory to wear a helmet on a trike, the Serrs prefer to do so. AUTHOR

The rocky southern end of Laxey Beach was the venue for a Sidecar Trial, scheduled to start at 6pm but delayed until 7pm when the tide was lower. The event was staged by the Southern MCC in collaboration with the Village Commissioners, who presented the winners' trophies.

The winning driver was Jake Kelly, whose father Roger Kelly was the Island's top trials and motocross rider in the Sixties. His passenger was 15 year old Ealish Baxter, whose older sister competes in the Ladies Trials World championship.

Winners Jake Kelly and Ealish Baxter (Beta). CHRIS MOLYNEUX

Graham's grit

Graham Crate from South Cheam in Surrey first visited the TT in 1978 and has been running his distinctive white BMW/Steib sidecar outfit for 27 years.

"I love this old bike but in 1987 I turned it over on the Druidale road and woke up in a helicopter with back, pelvis and head injuries," Graham says. "Recently I've been out of action after eye operations, but decided I really had to come back this year." AUTHOR

Results

Expert
1 Jake Kelly/Ealish Baxter (Beta) 5 marks lost
2 Adrian Smith/Aaron Smith (Gas Gas) 12
3 Mark Bimson/Jane Birchall (Sherco) 18

Clubman
1 Gerry Hannay/Paul Watterson (Beta) 17
2 Dougie Christian/Kevin Watterson (Gas Gas) 22
3 Brian Bedford/Stuart Bedford (Sherco) 36

Frustration. The weather's great, but the Mountain Road is closed following an accident. There were several total closures, which used to be very rare, during the TT period. LILY PUBLICATIONS

Leaving for home

This Moto Guzzi-mounted trio had to set off home to Tuscany before racing ended. Simone Fontini (left) and hill-climb racer Massimo 'Turbine' Tumminello met fellow Italian Carlo Dué (centre) at the Ace Café in London and joined forces for the TT trip, camping at the Glenlough site. Simone's trusty 1980 1000cc G5 had been voted Best in Show at the Guzzi Owners Club meet at the Shore Hotel, Laxey on Wednesday evening.
"This is biking heaven. I want to live here!" Carlo said as they departed on their three-day journey. AUTHOR

"This is my first time at the TT and I love to ride around the Course," enthused Germain Gonzalez, who made a four-day journey from Las Palmas in the Canary Islands on his Kawasaki Z750. AUTHOR

Italians invade

A fleet of 19 Moto Guzzi singles turned heads at the Vintage Motor Cycle Club's gathering in St John's. They belonged to members of a club for owners of classic Guzzis in Vicenza, Italy who had shipped their 500cc Falcone, Astore and GTV models to Dublin for a tour of the Isle of Man and Ireland. The riders were from the UK, USA and Switzerland as well as Italy. "The Isle of Man was stupendous – and such beautiful weather!" said Californian Guzzi fan Patrick Hayes, who rode a loaned machine with his wife Regina on the pillion.

In the afternoon, the VMCC riders visited Government House, where machines lined up for a display in which the Best in Show award was won by Mike Barry for his magnificent 1936 Coventry Eagle.

Patrick Hayes with loaned Guzzi Falcone Turismo.
TRACEY HARDING

Steve Colley in mid-manoeuvre, captured on one of the huge screens erected on Douglas Promenade. BERNARD WEBER

Peel Beach Cross

Masses of spectators lined the Peel Promenade railings to watch beach racing sponsored by Yamaha and Davison's Ice Cream. Staged by the Ramsey MCC, the event took place during the evening low tide. A collection for the Royal National Lifeboat Institution raised £800, while £100 went to St John Ambulance.

Results

Solos

1 Matthew Lund (Yamaha)
2 Gareth Quayle (Honda)
3 Will Keenan ((KTM)

Quads

1 Kev Coole (Suzuki)
2 Tom Collister (KTM)
3 Steve Ennett (Suzuki)

Quad mayhem set against a tranquil sea. FOTTOFINDERS

Martin rolls a Robin

Supersport lap record holder Guy Martin took part in a stock car race on the oval track at Onchan Raceway, driving a Reliant Robin three-wheeler. Taking an early lead he was passed and relegated to third. Coming back at the leaders he moved up second place and was trying hard to regain the lead when he turned his car over. Climbing out unhurt, Guy got a big cheer from the crowd.

Loyalty *awards*

An awards ceremony was held at the Empress Hotel in Douglas for TT fans who have attended the races regularly over the past decades. Tourism and leisure minister Adrian Earnshaw presented engraved tankards to 45 long-term TT supporters, including 92 year old Londoner Les Gilles who had not missed a TT, or a Manx GP, since 1947. Another of those honoured was Ken Sprayson, given a certificate to recognise the 50th anniversary of his free welding service to TT competitors.

Specialbrew

The Sulby Glen Hotel served an exclusive real ale during the TT period. Dunlop Draught The Next Generation was specially commissioned from Okells Brewery and proceeds from every pint went to the Manx Grand Prix Helicopter fund and to support young TT riders Michael and William from the famous Dunlop family. Rosie Christian, who runs the pub with her husband Eddie, is mother of Daniel Sayle, Sidecar TT passenger to Nick Crowe and formerly Dave Molyneux, and Matthew Sayle, who drove in his first Sidecar TT this year passengered by Finn Aki Aalto.

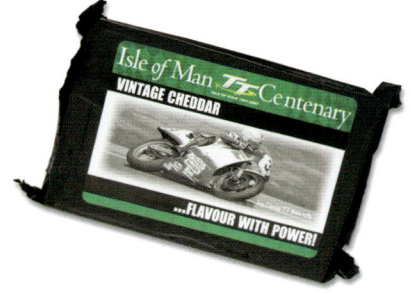

Another one bites the sand. BERNARD WEBER

130mph!
McGuinness
makes history

PokerStars **Senior TT**

The thoroughly professional John McGuinness did a magnificent job in the six-lap PokerStars Senior, both for himself, for Honda and for the 100 year old TT races. By winning, he raised his personal tally of TT victories to 13 and Honda's total to 133. And by breaking the 130mph lap speed barrier on his second circuit, he gave the Centenary a permanent marker. Just like Bob McIntyre's first 100mph lap in the Golden Jubilee TT of 1957, the achievement of the other 'Mac' fifty years later will stand as a Mountain Course racing milestone.

To average 130mph around the TT Course, with its 220-plus corners, its countless bumps, ripples, blind crests, kerbs and gutters is a staggering, almost superhuman achievement. And as John acknowledged after the historic race, it takes a team effort. He praised his powerful 1000cc machine, the HM Plant Honda squad who tended it and the grippy tailor-made tyres supplied by Dunlop.

"Absolutely brilliant," were his words at the finish. "When I went through Quarterbridge on the third lap, the whole crowd reared up. I'm so proud to have done it. I never imagined this when I was in a muddy hole laying bricks," he said, referring to the days when he worked as a bricklayer to raise funds for his racing.

The HM Plant Honda's rear wheel kicks up as Man of the Centenary John McGuinness speeds through Union Mills. **DOUBLE RED**

Hedge trimmer! Guy Martin takes a tight line through Tower Bends, between Waterworks and the Gooseneck. ADY GELL

Ian Hutchinson stays tucked in as his Honda rears up on the undulating descent from Kate's Cottage to Creg-ny-Baa. DOUBLE RED

Another bad day for Bruce Anstey. Suspension problems with the Suzuki forced him to give up after one lap. DOUBLE RED

His 13 TT wins put him in equal third ranking with Dave Molyneux, behind Joey Dunlop's 26 victories and Mike Hailwood's 14. To add to his lap at 130mph, more than seven seconds better than his previous 2006 record of 129.451mph, John hoisted the outright six-lap race average record to 127.255mph.

"On the first lap the road was a bit dusty in places. There were traces of oil spills at Sarah's Cottage and Guthrie's, then some swirling mist on the Mountain gave me a bit of a shock," John recounted. "But the tyres were working well and I really concentrated hard on that second lap. We had geared the bike a bit shorter (a lower ratio) today to gain acceleration."

Guy Martin, who finished second on his Hydrex Honda Fireblade as he had in the Superbike race, also rode magnificently and came tantalisingly close to hitting the iconic 130mph himself with a second lap at 129.816mph.

"Massive respect to John. A win next year, we hope," Guy said in the post-race interviews, explaining that he'd had a problem in the later stages.

"I wanted to pull John in, but the chain started jumping the sprocket in first gear and then in the higher gears as well and I thought 'oh my god!' I am so relieved to have finished. Our team have worked their nuts off all week."

Lacking the devastating speed of the leaders, Ian Lougher collected his best result of the week on the Stobart Honda. DOUBLE RED

Third man Ian Hutchinson (HM Plant Honda) was quiet and subdued compared with the ever-voluble Martin.

"I had to slow for yellow flags a couple of times. Once I realised I had a safe third place I stuck with that. I'm very pleased to have finished on the podium in all my four races," he said.

McGuinness led from the word go. Manx Radio's Glen Helen commentator Maurice Mawdsley reported that after the first nine miles he led Hutchinson by two seconds, with Martin, Ian Lougher, Bruce Anstey and Michael Rutter completing the top six.

Hutchinson, who tucks himself away aerodynamically on the bike, was reported as hitting 191mph through the Sulby speed trap. But by Ramsey Hairpin he was down to third behind Martin by nearly two seconds, while Super Mac had extended his lead to almost four seconds.

Two Irish hopes Ryan Farquhar (Mark Johns Honda) and Martin Finnegan (Alpha Boilers Honda) dropped out early with machine failures and Anstey was losing ground and clearly troubled. His Relentless by TAS Suzuki team mate Adrian Archibald was still going strong, but so was meteoric young Manxman Conor Cummins.

The outright lap record fell when McGuinness flashed across the line to start lap two and the near-instantaneous electronic timing indicated 129.883mph from a standing start and a lead of almost 10 seconds over Martin. Behind Hutchinson, Lougher was holding fourth place ahead of Cummins, Archibald and Rutter. Anstey, winner of Wednesday's Superstock race, pulled in to retire at the pits.

Ian Armstrong was ninth on a Yamaha sponsored by precision engineering company Canteen Smithy, collecting his fourth replica of the week. DOUBLE RED

"I got a tank-slapper on Bray Hill. There's something wrong with the suspension," he said, understandably dejected at his third disappointment of the week.

Loud cheers erupted from the packed grandstand when the 130mph lap was announced when McGuinness came in after lap two to refuel and change the rear tyre. As ever his pit crew got him away sharpish, but Martin and Hutchinson, who arrived at almost the same time as Rutter and Archibald, took longer.

Manx rider Nigel Beattie's stop went awry when the rear wheel refused to go in properly. Despairing, he got off the bike, but was urged to get back on by his pit crew and eventually set off, only to be forced to stop at Kirk Michael when a dislodged filler cap covered him in petrol.

Guy Martin was down on the leader by more than 20 seconds at Glen Helen, but clawed four of them back by Ramsey: he obviously excels on what is considered the toughest part of the Course. Lougher held on to fourth, with Archibald up to fifth ahead of Cummins after the pit stops. Behind them were Rutter and leading newcomer Steve Plater. Another fast first-timer, Scot Keith Amor, had retired when ninth.

On lap four Martin overhauled Hutchinson to lie second on the road as the leaders began to catch back markers. Steadying up for a lap at 129.296mph, McGuinness had another slick pit stop as did Martin this time, but Hutchinson's bike did not re-start instantly.

Steve Plater (AIM Yamaha) completed an excellent first TT with seventh place and a fourth silver replica. DOUBLE RED

Smooth-riding McGuinness sweeps through Stella Maris on the approach to Ramsey hairpin. LILY PUBLICATIONS

Former 125cc TT winner Chris Palmer (Yamaha) just missed a silver replica despite averaging more than 121mph and had to settle for bronze. STAN BASNETT

In total control, McGuinness maintained his lead over Martin for the final two laps, and the interval was more than 30 seconds at the chequered flag.

Lougher, top in the 2006 Duke Road Race Rankings, got his best result of the week in fourth as did Archibald in fifth. Conor Cummins took sixth place, regaining his 'fastest Manxman' status with a belting second lap at 126.466mph while Steve Plater capped off an excellent newcomer's week with seventh place at an average of 123.076mph and his fourth silver replica.

Michael Rutter finally managed to finish, explaining that after a rash of engine troubles he had run a standard ZX-10 road motor. Even so, his best lap was his fourth at 125.97mph, despite pain from his pre-TT wrist injury. A post-race X-ray revealed a broken bone.

Yorkshire's Ian Armstrong, carrying number 13 got the best of his four finishes at ninth. He found out after the race that his mechanic Steve 'Mantis' Gibson had his foot broken when a rider in an adjacent pit ran over it.

Roy Richardson from Blackpool, winner of three Manx GP Classic races, was the highest finisher on a 600cc machine (Yamaha R6), earning him the TT Supporters Club Trophy.

Braking for Creg-ny-Baa: James McBride from Kettering took his Speedfreak Racing Yamaha to tenth place. DOUBLE RED

Hutchinson closes on Relentless Suzuki rider Adrian Archibald at Ramsey Hairpin. They finished third and fourth respectively. LILY PUBLICATIONS

The gearbox in Steve Linsdell's Paton gave out on the third lap at Bishop's Court. He later pointed out that the two-stroke 500cc V-four had covered considerably more than the distance of a typical grand prix race.

John McGuinness, who collected £22,000 in prize money, hinted that he might retire after his historic performance. But he affirmed his support for Isle of Man TT racing, saying: "Let's keep this thing going for another 100 years!"

RIGHT
Rostrum antics. Third man Hutchinson sprays champagne in the winner's face and second finisher Guy Martin winces. DOUBLE RED

BELOW
Rob Barber flies the flag on a British-made Triumph. He took the three-cylinder Supersport class machine to 44th place. DOUBLE RED

PokerStars *Senior TT*

1	John McGuinness	H M Plant Honda	1h 46m 44.23s	127.255mph
2	Guy Martin	Hydrex Honda	1h 47m 16.96s	126.608mph
3	Ian Hutchinson	H M Plant Honda	1h 48m 04.60s	125.677mph
4	Ian Lougher	Stobart Honda	1h 49m 08.12s	124.458mph
5	Adrian Archibald	TAS Suzuki	1h 49m 21.61s	124.202mph
6	Conor Cummins	Millsport Yamaha	1h 49m 47.86s	123.708mph
7	Steve Plater	AIM Yamaha	1h 50m 21.67s	123.076mph
8	Michael Rutter	MSS Discovery Kawasaki	1h 50m 42.22s	122.695mph
9	Ian Armstrong	Canteen Smithy Yamaha	1h 51m 56.08s	121.346mph
10	James McBride	Yamaha	1h 51m 59.14s	121.290mph

ALL THE ABOVE RECEIVED SILVER REPLICAS

11	Chris Palmer	Solway Slate & Tile Yamaha	1h 52m 10.23s	121.091mph
12	Ian Pattinson	Martin Bullock Raceteam Suzuki	1h 52m 34.07s	120.663mph
13	Gary Carswell	Bolliger Kawasaki	1h 52m 44.30s	120.481mph
14	Mark Buckley	Crossan Motorcycles Suzuki	1h 52m 53.42s	120.319mph
15	Les Shand	Barron Transport Honda	1h 53m 35.52s	119.575mph
16	Gary Johnson	Speedfreak Racing Yamaha	1h 54m 16.91s	118.854mph
17	Mark Miller	Wolfman Padgetts Aprilia	1h 54m 25.46s	118.705mph
18	Stephen Oates	Hallett Aviation Suzuki	1h 54m 33.81s	118.561mph
19	Phil Stewart	Yamaha	1h 54m 34.42s	118.551mph
20	Paul Dobbs	Dave East Suzuki	1h 54m 44.70s	118.374mph
21	Stefano Bonetti	Suzuki	1h 55m 13.49s	117.881mph
22	Craig Atkinson	Martin Bullock Raceteam Suzuki	1h 55m 16.26s	117.834mph
23	Paul Shoesmith	Speedfreak Racing Yamaha	1h 55m 30.03s	117.600mph
24	Roy Richardson	Ian Barnes Racing Yamaha	1h 55m 49.30s	117.273mph
25	George Spence	Yamaha	1h 56m 07.52s	116.967mph
26	Adrian McFarland	Hardship Racing Yamaha	1h 56m 23.25s	116.703mph
27	Ian Mackman	Bill Smith Suzuki	1h 56m 42.24s	116.387mph
28	Tim Poole	Bill Smith Yamaha	1h 56m 47.37s	116.302mph
29	Paul Duckett	Wilson & Collins Kawasaki	1h 57m 01.17s	116.073mph
30	Thomas Schonfelder	ADAC Hessen-Thueringen Suzuki	1h 57m 03.55s	116.034mph
31	James Edmeades	Speedfreak Racing Yamaha	1h 57m 04.63s	116.016mph
32	John Crellin	J Richards Suzuki	1h 57m 14.73s	115.849mph

ALL THE ABOVE RECEIVED BRONZE REPLICAS

33	Stephen Harper	Suzuki	1h 57m 26.44s	115.657mph
34	William Dunlop	Lilley Racing Kawasaki	1h 57m 40.71s	115.423mph
35	David Paredes	Bill Smith Yamaha	1h 58m 03.03s	115.059mph
36	Fabrice Miguet	Suzuki	1h 58m 18.57s	114.807mph
37	Andrew Marsden	Yamaha	1h 58m 21.89s	114.754mph
38	Alan Connor	Dunshaughlin RRS Suzuki	1h 53m 30.85s	114.609mph
39	David Milling	Dave Milling Motorcycles Honda	1h 58m 44.42s	114.391mph
40	Alan Bud Jackson	BDS Fuels Suzuki	1h 59m 52.35s	113.310mph
41	Chris Petty	York Suzuki Centre Suzuki	2h 00m 03.16s	113.140mph
42	Derran Slous	Suzuki	2h 00m10.73s	113.022mph
43	Karsten Schmidt	Ducati	2h 00m 34.72s	112.647mph
44	Robert Barber	Triumph	2h 01m 51.36s	111.466mph
45	David Hewson	Kawasaki	2h 02m 20.01s	111.031mph
46	Etienne Godart	Martin Bullock Raceteam Honda	2h 03m 13.79s	110.223mph
47	Sandor Bitter	Suzuki	2h 03m 40.04s	109.834mph

FASTEST LAP: JOHN McGUINNESS – 17M 21.99S; 130.354MPH ON LAP THREE (NEW RECORD)
FIRST 600CC FINISHER ROY RICHARDSON, 24TH PLACE OVERALL

McGuinness acknowledges the crowd as he heads to the winners' enclosure. DAVE COLLISTER

With the historic Tourist Trophy. LILY PUBLICATIONS

Sign language. DOUBLE RED

The Motor Cycle News Parade of Champions

Rod Gould, 1970 250cc world champion, prepares to take off on a 350cc Yamaha two-stroke. LILY PUBLICATIONS

The centenary TT's grand finale was a Mountain Course parade reserved for the very famous. Before it started, autograph hunters ran amok in the paddock assembly area, grabbing the rare opportunity of having so many big names together in one place.

Carl Fogarty, Britain's most famous motorcycle racer since Barry Sheene, was celebrating the fifteenth anniversary of his 1992 123.61mph TT Course lap record, that stood for seven years. His parade mount was an MV Agusta F1000R, similar to machines that will be run in the company's 2008 World Superbike campaign, managed by Fogarty.

Charismatic Giacomo Agostini, on a flying two-day visit from Italy, rode a 500cc three-cylinder MV of the type he raced 40 years ago, loaned by the Elli collection. The ten-times TT winner, who decided not to race on the Mountain Course after 1972, has been a regular TT visitor in recent years.

"It's too long! I cannot believe how anyone can memorise that," Noriyuki Haga.

Chas Mortimer, winner of eight TTs from 1970 to 1978, screams off the line on a 250cc Yamaha. AUTHOR

A 500cc MV Four from earlier times was ridden by John Surtees, winner of six TTs between 1956 and 1960. The only man to have won the premier world championships on two and four wheels, he has kept his faith with the motorcycling world.

Phil Read was one of the TT's harshest critics in the early Seventies but ate his words and returned to take his last of 8 wins in 1977. Now a regular at TT parades, he was loaned a 500cc Kay Gilera Four replica.

Phillip McCallen was on a Honda RC45, the model that took him to five of his eleven TT victories between 1992 and 1997 and similar V-fours were paraded by other Nineties' Honda stars, Ian Simpson and Iain Duffus.

Charlie Williams had a 1980 250cc two-stroke of the Yamaha brand on which he won nine TT races and seven-times winner Chas Mortimer rode the Yamaha Classic Racing Team's fabulous 250cc two-stroke four. Also Yamaha-mounted was Rob McElnea, lap record breaker at 117mph on a Suzuki in 1984 and now in charge of Yamaha's UK racing campaigns.

Graeme Crosby (three wins, 1980-1981) tried his special-edition Suzuki GSX-R1000 out round the Course and six-times winner Jim Redman, 75 and coping with a painful hip, was lent a HM Plant 1000cc Honda Superstock. Chester dealer Bill Smith, who started in 86 races from 1957 to 2001 and won four, was aboard the 1978 900cc Hailwood Ducati.

"I went into the straw bales at Waterworks and fell off," Barry Smith

Scot Iain Duffus, who won two TTs in the Nineties burns the tyre on a borrowed Blacks Bike Shop Suzuki. DAVE COLLISTER

Typical Fogarty! The four-times World Superbike champion wheelies his MV Agusta. DAVE COLLISTER

Giacomo Agostini winner of ten TTs from 1966 to 1972 can still do an elegant run-and-bump start on his 500cc MV Agusta. AUTHOR

Brian Dunill, a TT spectator since 1966, shows his colour action tattoos of Mike Hailwood and Giacomo Agostini. AUTHOR

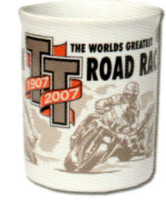

Eleven times TT winner Phillip McCallen from Northern Ireland 'out for a wee ride round' on a 180bhp Honda RC45.
STAN BASNETT

Fresh from his Senior triumph John McGuinness rode a Honda RC45. He had been prevented from parading a Joey Dunlop-type 2000 Honda SP-1 in the Dunlop Lap of Honour on a technicality, so Honda did not field the big twin with Ron Haslam aboard in the MCN event, as had been planned.

Thirteen-times Sidecar winner Dave Molyneux, a lifelong admirer of Seventies charioteer George O'Dell, built a replica of the Yamaha TZ750-powered Windle outfit on which O'Dell lapped at 102mph in 1977. He took it on a noisy lap, accompanied by O'Dell's former passenger Kenny Arthur, now 63. The pair even wore 1977-style Shell leathers, made for the occasion by Manx Leathers.

Famous guest riders who had not raced at the TT were also in the parade. They were Yamaha's popular World Superbike contender Noriyuki Haga, Island resident and former World Superbike champion Neil Hodgson and British Superbike star John Reynolds.

Some machines only completed partial laps. Mitsui Itoh's 50cc Suzuki started from Creg-ny-Baa and Luigi Taveri pulled the 125cc Honda off at Braddan as he had on Tuesday. Stuart Graham managed a full lap on the replica Honda six, pushing in after a tumble at Governor's.

Foggy, who'd set off at Number 1 pulling a gigantic wheelie, was also the first to complete a lap. "That brought back great memories," he said, grinning, and as the other paraders arrived back, they too were all smiles.

Former World Superbike champion Neil Hodgson rides the Mountain Course on closed roads for the first time, on a 750cc Honda RC30.
TRACEY HARDING

Mitsui Itoh    Graeme Crosby    Carl Fogarty    Luigi Taveri    Rob McElnea    Giacomo Agostini    Philip McCallen    Mick Grant

"I thoroughly enjoyed that!" Kenny Arthur, after passengering Dave Molyneux on the O'Dell replica.

ABOVE
Rob Fisher, 10-times winner of sidecar TTs from 1994 to 2002, passengered by Mick Wynn on a 350cc Yamaha F2 outfit. AUTHOR

RIGHT
Dave Molyneux on his George O'Dell Yamaha replica. The feet belong to O'Dell's one-time passenger Kenny Arthur. AUTHOR

"That was very enlightening. I'd forgotten just how bumpy it is. The enthusiasm shown by people around the Course was tremendous," John Surtees.

Kenny Arthur   John Surtees   Michael Rutter   Noriyuki Haga   Jim Redman   Barry Smith   Dave Molyneux   John McGuinness

Tragedy on the Mountain

News of a terrible accident in the latter stages of the Senior race put a damper on rejoicing at the first 130mph lap. Newcomer Marc Ramsbotham (34) from Wymondham, Norfolk lost control of his Suzuki GSX-R1000 at the 26th Milestone (also known as Joey's) on the Mountain climb and was killed instantly. His machine hit four people. Dean Adrian Jacob (33) from Kidderminster, a spectator, died at the scene and another spectator Gregory John Kenzig (52) from Queensland Australia died despite attempts to revive him in Noble's Hospital. Two marshals were injured: Janice Phillips from Ramsey was detained in Noble's for several days and former TT rider Hilary Musson, who lives in Ballaugh, was in the hospital's intensive therapy unit for a month following the incident.

Marc Ramsbotham rounds the Gooseneck. It was less than a mile further on up the Mountain that he crashed and was killed along with two spectators. Riding in his first Mountain Course meeting, 'Rammy' was a well-liked rider who had achieved fine results at Dundrod in Ireland and Oliver's Mount, Scarborough. ADY GELL

Packing up for home. AUTHOR

Senior Yamaha engineers in the paddock. Takashi Mitsui LEFT designer of the early Seventies' 500cc four and chassis for the Sixties' 125cc and 250cc fours with Taichi Ito, who developed 500cc fours ridden by Giacomo Agostini and Kenny Roberts. He is now a Yamaha communications chief. AUTHOR

Vendors selling tee-shirts, hats and other TT merchandise reported brisk sales and in some cases stocks ran out.
TRACEY HARDING

Badge baron. A familiar sight at the TT, Konrad 'Konni' Ammenhäuser works for a bank in Marburg, Germany.
LILY PUBLICATIONS

Great turnout for a tiny marque. A dozen CRS owners from Italy and the USA ended the week with a gathering at the home of Manx resident Paul Mercer. AUTHOR

Cummins, King

Conor Cummins holds the lead from Chris Palmer and Ian Lougher in the 1000cc Steam Packet race. DAVE COLLISTER

Record crowds lined the Billown Circuit for the Steam Packet Company National Road Races. The Saturday post-TT meeting was started in 1991 to entertain racing fans unable to leave the Isle of Man directly after the Senior TT because of heavy ferry bookings. It is promoted by the Southern 100 Club which organises the principal Billown event in July.

Conor Cummins, who had ridden brilliantly on the Mountain Course, shone in the Steam Packet races as well, winning the main 1000cc event on his Millsport Yamaha. He comfortably beat Billown expert Chris Palmer, also on a

Yamaha, and seasoned real roads maestro Ian Lougher on his Black Horse Honda.

The combined 125cc/400cc race was won overall by Palmer on a 125cc Mannin Collections Honda. Winner of the two last Ultra Lightweight TTs before the 125cc class was dropped for 2005, he headed the other two-strokes of former TT star Robert Dunlop and Dan Sayle, Nick Crowe's Sidecar TT passenger. New Zealander Paul Dobbs was second overall to top the 400cc class for the second consecutive year.

In the opening 250cc/600cc race, there was a third-lap incident

# of Billown
Saturday 9 June

Close dicing through Ballabeg. The rider looking back is Roy Richardson, fastest 600cc rider in yesterday's Senior TT. DAVE COLLISTER

at the Cross Four Ways corner in which four spectators were injured as well as a rider. It was a grim echo of dreadful events on the Mountain the day before, but mercifully there were no life-threatening injuries. After Carl Roberts fell off his 250cc Honda, it kept going and eventually hit the spectators, who were behind a barrier, as it came to a stop. The race was stopped while the injured were taken to Nobles Hospital and re-started as a six-lapper after 40 minutes.

This time, Lougher (Honda) headed Cummins (Yamaha) while the fastest lap – a 600cc class record – was set by Yamaha rider Adrian McFarland at 105.883mph. Another Northern Irishman, William Dunlop (Honda), won the 250cc class.

Steam Packet Road Races – Results

RACE 1 250CC TWO-STROKES/600CC FOUR-STROKES (SIX LAPS)
1	Ian Lougher	600 Black Horse Honda
2	Conor Cummins	600 Millsport Yamaha
3	Adrian McFarland	600 Hardship Racing Yamaha

250CC CLASS WINNER: WILLIAM DUNLOP (FLYNN HONDA), 12TH OVERALL
FASTEST LAP: ADRIAN MCFARLAND – 105.883MPH (NEW CLASS RECORD)

RACE 2 125CC TWO-STROKES/500CC FOUR-STROKES (SIX LAPS)
1	Chris Palmer	125 Mannin Honda
2	Paul Dobbs	400 Yamaha (400cc class winner)
3	Mark Parrett	400 Honda

FASTEST LAP: PAUL DOBBS – 96.441MPH (NEW CLASS RECORD)

RACE 3 1000CC (NINE LAPS)
1	Conor Cummins	1000 JMF Millsport Yamaha
2	Chris Palmer	1000 Solway Yamaha
3	Ian Lougher	1000 Black Horse Honda

FASTEST LAP: CONOR CUMMINS – 108.786MPH

Peace returns to Kirk Michael village. Much of the special racing furniture is left in position until after the late-summer Manx Grand Prix. LILY PUBLICATIONS

After the Centenary

As the last TT visitors left, the Isle of Man was left to reflect on the Centenary TT.

Normal service resumed. The busy Mountain route between Douglas and Ramsey reverted to two-way traffic. LILY PUBLICATIONS

There was shock and sadness at the triple deaths on the Mountain, which happened in the closing stages of the last race, just when things looked set for a fatality-free TT. It was the first time in 100 years that TT spectators were killed and the incident will no doubt lead to a serious study of no-go areas alongside the Course. There are already many, but sometimes members of the public remove the Prohibited Area signs. Marshals will have to take a tougher line and we could yet see the start of a TT race delayed while a single individual is persuaded to move from a particular spot.

Away from the racing, the Manx police reported a sharp decrease in serious and fatal accidents on the Mountain Road, despite a small rise in the number of collisions and a massive increase in traffic. During the fortnight one visiting motorcyclist was killed in a collision off the TT Course.

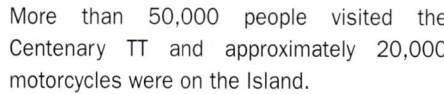

Freshly printed. Dot Tilbury of IoM Post shows off the latest issue of TT stamps.
LILY PUBLICATIONS

More than 50,000 people visited the Centenary TT and approximately 20,000 motorcycles were on the Island.

The 2007 TT was judged an overall success, helped by predominantly fine weather, spectacularly fast racing, hard work put in by many on the Island and the enthusiasm pumped into the many support events. There were some complaints, mainly about over-priced food and accommodation, as well as much-publicised discontent with the ferry service. The Manx government has promised to investigate the Steam Packet's operations and fares policy.

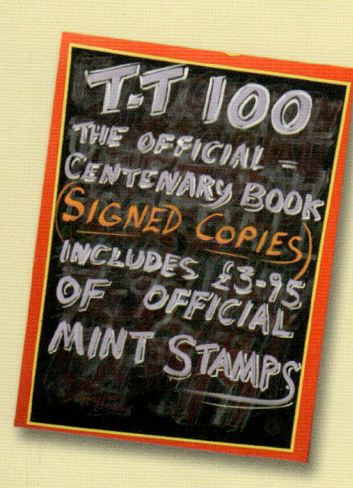

Murray Walker found time in his frantic schedule to sign copies of TT100, the official history of the races for which he wrote the Foreword. He is at the Lexicon Bookshop in Strand Street, Douglas and proprietor David Ashworth stands behind him. BARRY EDWARDS

Ronaldsway Airport had a busy TT period with an aircraft movement every three minutes at peak times. This Titan Airways Boeing 737 was chartered by Honda. BARRY EDWARDS

Not quite a Gatwick queue, but 24,000 passengers passed through Ronaldsway at TT time.
BARRY EDWARDS

What of **the future?**

Although 2008 is bound to be quieter, the Centenary will have made new TT converts who will return, if not every year. There could be a boost for 2009 when Honda celebrates its 50 years of TT participation, while 2011 is a major milestone: the 100th anniversary of motorcycle racing over the Mountain. Further ahead, 2020 will be the 100th TT to be held since 1907.

Whatever the occasion, for many the actual racing is fundamental to successful TTs. Over-subscribed grids and a high standard of riding showed a continuing healthy trend in 2007 and the TT Marshals Association is working hard to maintain their numbers, on which everything depends. Keeping the bigger teams happy is always difficult for the organisers, but their presence is vital in maintaining the TT's prestige.

The perennial issue of safety will continue to loom large. Riders accept the risks of TT racing, but when spectators are killed it's a different matter. We must hope ways can be found to keep the unique Mountain Course viable, at least until 2020.

Cheeky girls! DAVE COLLISTER

Boarding the ferry home. Continental riders need to organise their travel around two sea crossings. LILY PUBLICATIONS